Floating on Solitude

BOOKS BY DAVE SMITH

Poetry

Floating on Solitude (1996)

Fate's Kite: Poems, 1991–1995 (1995)

Night Pleasures: New and Selected Poems (1992)

Cuba Night (1990)

The Roundhouse Voices: Selected and New Poems (1985)

Gray Soldiers (1984)

In the House of the Judge (1983)

Homage to Edgar Allan Poe (1981)

Dream Flights (1981)

Blue Spruce (1981)

Goshawk, Antelope (1979)

In Dark, Sudden with Light (1977)

Cumberland Station (1976)

Drunks (1975)

The Fisherman's Whore (1974, 1993)

Mean Rufus Throw Down (1973)

Bull Island (1970)

Fiction

Southern Delights (1984)

Onliness (1981)

Criticism

The Essential Poe (1991)

Local Assays: On Contemporary American Poetry (1985)

The Pure Clear Word: Essays on the Poetry of James Wright (1982)

Anthologies

New Virginia Review 8 (1991)

New Virginia Review 4 (1986)

The Morrow Anthology of Younger American Poets (1985)

Floating
on Solitude

THREE VOLUMES OF POETRY BY

Dave Smith

University of Illinois Press

Urbana & Chicago

Manufactured in the United States of America

P 5 4 3 2 I

This book is printed on acid-free paper.

Floating on Solitude combines *Cumberland Station* (1976),
Goshawk, Antelope (1979), and *Dream Flights* (1981),
all previously published by the University of Illinois Press.

Library of Congress Cataloging-in-Publication Data

Smith, Dave, 1942–

Floating on solitude : three volumes of poetry / by Dave Smith.

p.   cm.

ISBN 0-252-06584-0 (pbk. : alk. paper)

I. Title.

PS3569.M5173F56   1996

811'.54—dc20   96-9967

                    CIP

ON THE COVER:

"Workboats Abandoned and Sunk by Watermen, Poquoson,
Virginia." Photo by Dave Smith, 1970.

The fate of man is to be the ever-recurrent, reproachful

Eye floating upon the night and solitude.

—Loren Eisely, *The Unexpected Universe*

TO DEE SMITH

With love and because

she helped make this book,

word by word

WAITING FOR DEE IN THE DINER

Clacked on the cheap china, our forks,
      knives barely cut the blare
of voices, those passing out to work,
      those waiting—summers, winters,

lives weaved by whoever brought eggs,
      white gravy, bread married
to blood-colored jam, coffee's dregs
      bitter, hot as the steamed

cries from small rooms of our houses.
      Some here paid, didn't return,
and we told their tales, kept count
      of the days as long as we could.

Then forgot why we watched the door,
      howled at a line once said
like *that*. We pretended to answers,
      then the quiet. Homes we had

changed colors like hair, added rooms.
      No one now calls, "Hey Blondie!"
Lies I told here in pride and gloom
      turned to truth, and fear.

Still, we took this road. Now come
      fine iron days remembered,
men, women, our hungers and loves,
      the always last, hushed *forever*.

CONTENTS

Between 1973 and 1981 I wrote many poems. No one does creative work of any quantity or durable quality without the help of others who, themselves, receive no public recognition. It would be impossible to list all those who made these books not merely possible but also literal events, and my gratitude has grown throughout the years for a support more valuable than ever. It is invidious to name only a few, but I must say my special thanks to certain noble editors, among them the late Howard Moss, Arthur Vogelsang, Larry Lieberman, and Dick Wentworth, and to the poets Norman Dubie and Stephen Dunn.

When this reprint volume of three original books was first proposed to me, it was suggested that I write a preface. I did not then and do not now know what would be pertinent or interesting except perhaps this: I grew up among the tidal marshes of Virginia where men had made a living for nearly several hundred years by becoming what they called a "waterman." This meant, usually, that a man bought a workboat, hired a helper if he did well, then spent some fifty to seventy years working the waters of the Chesapeake Bay and its tributaries. He set, baited, and harvested crab pots and fish nets; he planted oyster seeds and then tonged the harvest. It was a lonely, dangerous, hard, and unglorious life that always seemed to me as grand and proud and mysterious as the lives of the mythical heroes our books praise. When a life was finished the family sometimes sold the boat. But often the boat was driven aground on a spot familiar to, maybe loved by, the deceased—where others riding water in or out might see the boat, and see its man in the mind's eye.

I thought then and think now of the obligation in poems as the sacramental nod of that recognition. The reader will find my poems move inland, too, but the ceremonies are scarcely changed, nor is the poet's obligation. That is, I think, to tell whatever truth we can with what love we bear. Readers should know these poems are printed exactly as they were first published, although some have been reprinted in revised form elsewhere.

Cumberland Station

To My Family, This Book

Above children, over the herd
of plastic animals, the armaments,
our angel keeps its shy place.
Something of its silence works
to ease our daily discontents.
Mostly, though, it waits.
We hardly look at it.

We call it *thing*. It hovers,
tucked tight as the lightning
bug in our fists, stilled
as we are in sometime fevers.
I touch it now for one who sings,
the woman who scoffs at angels,
yet nailed up the thing.

The Seamen call it *looming*. Philosophy is as yet in the rear of the seamen, for so far from having accounted for it, she has not given it a name. Its principal effect is to make distant objects appear larger, in opposition to the general law of vision, by which they are diminished. I knew an instance at Yorktown, from whence the water prospect eastwardly is without termination, wherein a canoe with three men, at a great distance was taken for a ship with its three masts.

—Thomas Jefferson, *Notes on the State of Virginia*

PART I

Alone in the camp, all others dumb
with the humming sleep of the reeds
and the dew so thick in their hair
it flashes like brilliant insects,
I get up and go down to the river.

The current skeins the bottom stones
with pale, early light, the cold flow
that cries to the seaborne salmon
come, my friend, come and be still.
In the earth, tree roots are listening.

Taking two stones I pound my shirt
like a woman whose knees are slick
after long kneeling; the arms float
away from me and the chest swells.
It is that easy to begin a passage.

Later I sit naked, clothing the trees
with shirt and pants that want wind.
It is then across water a wolverine
comes to drink and a trout dimples
the silence like the soul rising. I

begin to hear not far away the crash
of dammed water and a beaver's bark.
I think unaccountably of an early snow,
children with black, hungry eyes, men
cutting arrows where the elders bud.

An old cottonwood has jeweled, my piece
the bruise of a warrior's first spear
hurtled, retrieved as the sun circles
and a boy hardens to a man.
I touch it to see him learn the art
of killing, and a man grows
to a boy in the presence of scars.

It does not live, on my desk,
in its warm grains, would not burn,
though it is filled with smoke,
or slowly bear the agonizing green
of a desert spring. But as heartwood
I keep it for its weight, its shape
showing where the lance entered
and currents of sap loosed, shone,
broke the winter bark each year

as a man and a boy run down an arroyo
illusory with heat, tufts of dust
growing under their feet, the haze
of spring spreading like a sweat.
My finger sees the spear cocked
up like a bird toward the horizon
and I know the angle is still wrong
where a man grins up at the light
leaves, his arms open as if to soar,
and I feel the gouged bark fall, and
fall again, already beginning to be
mine, a spice in the dry air.

FIRST HUNT AT SMITHFIELD
For Harry M. Cornwell

Pulling in we're careful to be quiet, don't shut
doors, ease everything, careful as we cock
the Winchesters. No good, the farmer's bitch licks
a chain of barks, dirty chickens sound the alert.
                          You smoke. He's
up anyway because it's never early for a man
whose skin wakes without the lie of clocks.

A black snake slithers off the road we take,
his muscles ticking dew.
                    To me, to you, is it the same
high weaving green, boil of yellows, black trunks of oak?
Where our road ends you angle off, camouflaged
almost, and almost hang like an aging leaf
under the eddying light, a shadow on that slope.
I hardly hear you whisper *here* but feel
my buttocks take the rotting trunk. What words
I had to bite back, thousands it seemed.

You sweep the air like a hawk and load.

I know you'll calculate my shots, my time, unbreak
your father's double, portion out the shells. Will I
do it right? So many things to think about,
each one my need to please you.
                          I watched the gray
creep in a fickle drift at your temple. I made
my eyes track the trees like yours. I learned

each knob, each distant sound, the way morning heat
tricked the wet leaves to sing with snapping, how

one shape implies a family, a line in wait.

               The guns bent my bones
when you were done. It was a long road back.
You dumped their bodies in a pile. Cold water
washed the tufts of fur from my small knife. Later
you tendered the farmer meat and smoked a while
on the step of his truck. What you said was gone
before I heard it. I watched for that deep act
to pass between us, not knowing what it was. Dreaming

the dingy sinews of all those guts, the nights
played the same tune until I knew you well. I always
scrubbed the guns when we got home, made coffee
below the stairs, until your chair
stopped rocking, and your snore.

THE ANCESTOR

For Asham Buckner

How well I know him, old soldier in blue
Union suit that might have been fireman's show
duds on the day they burned the whorehouse down.
Captain of the hosing team, he sprayed crowds,
the settees, the porch, but let others scorch
handlebars and muttonchops. Not his torch.
He'd be damned, maybe, but he'd sin enough,
death, fire, and fear, too, at Antietam's bluffs.
Under him, I lie in Grandfather's house,
bird-fat for holidays, deep-sick of grouse,
television news, lies, repeated rapes
by puffing gents without girls, knowing ropes
bounce the way they always did, but more, worse.
Framed over faces that mumble this day's curse,
his face, distant as a moon, scarred, boot-scuffed,
but oddly close, a face that still spits, gruffs,
sits straight, that brittle god with bad back pain,
gut-shot by the past, present, future, flames
brazing each brass button. Our whores have names.
Brothers, fathers look up for his signals
but cold Buck's locked hard dumb in his Eagles.

WITH WALT WHITMAN AT FREDERICKSBURG

After Louis Simpson

I have brought the twittering flags old bear hug,
the swaying noose you admired at the end
of the 13th Brooklyn muskets sashaying
down Broadway, everybody's intended girl
swooning, Jesus, for the grandeur of it.

I have brought a tumbler of spring water
for the sipping if your brother George lives.

I see you and Simpson stepping carefully through
wreckage, the hacked-off arms, useless with Masonic
rings, for God's sake, shining like used-car lots.
The arms are so American, like parts junked
before the expiration of their longevity.
This is no joke for Velsor Brush to peddle.

I have brought a red handkerchief
for our mouths. God-almighty, the stink grows.

I've come here like you to pick a way to the heart
of the business, tracing out what ripples I can,
skirting blood pooled like knocked-over
coffee on my own sunny back porch. But
I see you and Simpson arm wrestling
in a lantern's moon, sighing out
the lonely words of America's losses.

I wish I could say it was December 13, 1862,
but the faces of young men I see aren't Christ,
dead and divine, and brother of all, though
they wear the green clothes of Park Rangers,
the polite smile of Toledo, and one
thinks you sold him a Buick.

Isn't it for them we threw the noose in a can?
I gave George's water to a small boy found
by his mother in time, the life saved
he thought lost, which he will lose again.

If you lay your body down in this Virginia green,
you feel the quick shadows of tourists, the whispers
that zing in your stomach like minié balls or
knee-high bees. Loafing like this
you can hear the freeway moaning under ground
dry and beige as freeze-shrunken coffee,
or look up into the drained, tossing leaves
of October. Alone on a stolen army blanket

I've stretched out a long time here
to dig from a bright afternoon the glazed eyes
of anyone whose temple, as I touch it to clean
away the smear of ice, breaks my heart.

At dusk I may be the only one left to drift
down Marye's Heights where the Rappahannock mist rolls
over rocks humped like bodies, little dunes
inside which a black tide I cannot see
goes on rising and falling. I want

to tell you how progress has not changed us much.
You can see breaking on the woods the lights
of cars and the broken limbs glow
in the boomed rush of traffic that chants
wrong, wrong, wrong, wrong.

The big steel tourist shield says maybe
fifteen thousand got it here. No word
of either Whitman or one uncle
I barely remember in the smoke
that filled his tiny mountain house.

If each finger were a thousand of them
I could clap my hands and be dead
up to my wrists. It was quick
though not so fast as we can do it
now, one bomb, atomic or worse,
one silly pod slung on wing-tip,
high up, an egg cradled
by some rapacious mockingbird.

Hiroshima canned nine times their number
in a flash. Few had the time
to moan or feel the feeling
ooze back in the groin.

In a ditch I stand
above Marye's Heights, the book-bold
faces of Brady's fifteen-year-old
drummers, before battle, rigid
as August's dandelions
all the way to the Potomac
rolling in my skull.

If Audubon came here, the names
of birds would gush, the marvel
single feathers make
evoke a cloud, a nation,
a gray blur preserved
on a blue horizon, but

there is only a wandering child,
one dark stalk snapped off
in her hand, held out to me.
Taking it, I try to help her
hold its obscure syllables
one instant in her mouth,
like a drift of wind
at the forehead, the front door,
the black, numb fingernails.

Ponderous, hanging in that bricked
circle, lord of cobblestones,
where the city's grit flecks,

the horseman seems to be running
a country's life, sword naked,
horse heroic, kicking free.

But someone has stuck like a bib
a note under his brass breast.
Or is it only the eviction

paper of a woman who cannot swallow
magnolias and eat muffins
any longer? Yellowed,

crisp as the early letters
which were months reaching those
at home with the good news

of freedom, it offends
in the craw of the Monument
Street crowd. They will extend

new efforts with sighs unmuffled.
That is one way to see it.
Another way is that of shuffling

collar up to the James River,
to blazing barrels and lies
older than Camptown races. There

the poster eye of a dark trotter
nailed to a gray-splintered wall
winks over a bottle.

In this picture you will see
Big Stone Gap, Virginia, the white
petals of dogwood blurred back
of the woman standing in what
we call the nave. She lifts
the snake, a moccasin, mouth pure
as cream when it opens, the shade
of Daddy's inner thigh. It ought
to be a rattler, big diamonds
chaining her throat like beads,
a tail to shake hell out of those
windows that overlook nothing.
But it's only black, thick
as horse cock in her little fingers,
its tongue licking the silence
out of the rough pews. You can't
buy rattlers anymore, big dozers
drove them away to prairies and
the snatching hands of farm boys
in sweat-belted baseball hats.
Times change, even way in here.
One cottonmouth per Sunday now,
bless the Lord for his bounty.
Three for Easter and Christmas.

FOR THE POLIOED GIRL KILLED BY
COTTONMOUTHS ON HER BIRTHDAY
d. May 1960, Virginia Beach, Virginia

On her birthday in the green-glowing May of each year
I hobble in my head to that ocean-side carnival
where she is screaming near the thrash
of winter's last indifferent surf,

close my eyes and one stunningly
soft face in my brain's room stands up,
comes alive with the fuse of birthday candles,
glows incandescent with a beauty nothing can snuff out.

I stand ghostly behind parents I can never see, unseen,
they who placed their three-years-living child
in the heart of a split-hoofed, musically
metal stallion, strapped her down

that she might never fly wildly
with her own loosed heart. Again the nod
to one who controls a lever, who sets teeth in
motions like the great gears of almighty God. Again I

must see her eyes widen with the slow planetlike sail
of that iron paddock plate, again,
convulsively hooked deep in her breath,
feel skull powder and powerful hurt flood her

veins like the backsurge of oceans tumbling down and
through the nerves of suddenly terrified
swimmers. Clenching her child, I
still hear the woman whisper, *It's only fear, only fear.*

Around and around she rides posing for a bulb's flash,
no leverage in this world enough to help her
unsay what she had not yet learned to
fear, their words: *She'll live*

all summer on this, on her body's
joy flying, will take on delight's blood
buoyant shape of fish, duck, and vaulting horse.
They said let her go, after church that soft Sunday,

on the first day of her fourth year. Even in her prayers
what could be better for a girl than a canter?
Oh, the fear that whirled in that heart!
Each year I feel despair bite

with its lifesaving needle-
teeth up and down her useless legs,
legs shackled to stand if only someone will
hold her two tiny arms up, feel her flesh try to say

how it needs help to stand suddenly on rubber bones
that cannot run from the thousand snakes
that all winter no one has prayed
into church. Useless despair,

for we know father-shriek but not
how to reach out in May for a mild girl
caught, trapped in surf-thunder and the easy
wheel of love whose horse circles blindly by the sea.

Not mother or father or lover of the woman she was not
ever to be, I do not know even her name or
why a nest of snakes came to live
near a child's tiny stable. If

I call it an accident of spring,
a sad, blind misunderstanding of cold-blooded
beings hungry for the joy of their young, a woman-
child still doomed, refuses to throw off bindings, to get

up by the sea with sea wind in her hair and flee poison
meaner than the teeth-sucking joy-boys who
caretake the levers and gears of God's
dumb designs. What then? Something

so hideous of intent it must fester
in mud-stink and be unknown to a self-steeled
father striking shot after shot to hold onto his love
for his first girl come to ride out the day of her birth?

Tonight, not even the anniversary of that time when she
sagged for joy, fear-pierced, spun loose from
her life, another child screams, dying
maybe for snakebite or bad legs

or Daddy. As stranger I throb
with that hurt tonight, every night, and
I lift my fist in the air like spring's rebellion
in May for children no man, no God loves enough to save.

You cannot get him easily, or you can so
easily what you get will be hardly
anything you'd want.

What you would wheedle for, of course, is
one with blood, a pulse in the throat,
claws that could cuddle eggs

or slice off the nails of your yellow toes.
To coax a thing like that from an air
rampant with colors like a cloak

worn, maybe, by a pedagogue or a pope
requires that you have sifted your stock
item by item and have found

no stance but respect for his escapability.
Oh, you could take a scatter-gun approach
for a lot of meat and feathers

or adopt a bigger bird and cross your fingers.
There are many who advocate both,
and some that sigh "Oh, hell"

as they gayly trot out their personal butchers:
poisoned heartmeat, traps like existence
with cul-de-sacs and tiny bells

to wake them up should anything be caught.
Many merely hunt, never knowing where.
If you like soft hours this

crowd's for you. The best sift dung and may
work years alone without a clue.
Then: the shadow, a fine

phrase in high fir, slight beating of a heart,
shift of a seed on a summer's day,
and all doubt

dissolves, as a taste of gun steel in your mouth
leaves Truth. That is when work begins,
the real, winds, hours, the lies

you crack like pretzels for an emperor of air.
What it will get you mostly is dead
and few who'll pull your boots.

Nobody knows exactly when it fell off the map
or what the pressures were on its flooding river.
The hedge, the tottering mailbox were gone. That dimple
of light from the bicycle that raised itself to creak
at noon across a clattering bridge names my father.
His blood silent as a surging wish drags this town
lost through my body, a place I can get back to only
by hunch and a train whistle that was right on time.

But time and trains were never right in Green Springs,
West Virginia. What color could map the coal's grime,
shacks shored against the river every March, mail
left to rot because no one answered to "Occupant"?
Farmers low on sugar cursed heat and left bad cigars
boys would puff back to clouds where they dreamed
of girls naked as their hands under outfield flies.
Scores were low. There were no springs for the sick.
Women lined their walls with the Sears catalog, but
the only fur they ever had was a warbled rabbit.
To get here think of dirt, think of night leaking,
the tick of waterbugs, a train held in Pittsburgh.

THE LUMINOSITY OF LIFE
After Doris Ullman

All the mothers and fathers here in sickness,
in health, in Ullman's black-and-whites
pretend not to be dying. *Where are they?*

Look close at the head against the hickory,
that man who lies at the picnic's end
by his wife on their best bedsheet,
their eyes feigning sleep, closed.

When did that happen? Who are they?
They are about to wake up and father you.

What about the river they crossed? The same,
hardening somewhere, become a new road.

*A certain light evokes itself, some distress
they never escape—you can't deny this.*
Yes, it plays like the distant chords of banjos
tickling in a sleeper's dream

                     and, as Ullman saw,
endless, begun. Light on those child-mothers,
the roccoco coils of the weather-withered
boardinghouse in Tuscaloosa.

                    *But who
speaks for that man about to crumple
backward when the chair legs break, the sun topples?*
The fat woman, naked in the top corner window.

The silk in her lap, lustrous somehow (*Please?*),
somehow knows, doesn't give a damn for tomorrow,
which pretends it isn't ever coming back.

Every face in this land knows what a lie is.

Your fat wife weeps through her yellow shawl.
By bricks furred with soot your ragged cat laps
from a bottle then darts down the alley as if kicked.
The foreman cradles a clipboard with your name,
counting numbers from doors stained, God knows,
beyond any human use. The forklift yammers,

see, as I relive this moment of a morning
like a room full of machines suddenly stopped.
Today is Friday is what we learn fifty times
each year in the safety lecture and your name heads
the list of who gets reamed. You giggle, *Zero*

defects is a prayer. The foreman's insults
tell us ice means a man needs more than good treads,
for Christ's sake, and blind fools cling to beds
of whores. Get some sleep, protect your eyes
with company lenses. We're engineered.

What happened to you? I don't know who I'm telling
how in last night's movie the words betrayed
the lips so I thought of lathes knocked out
of their smooth pigeon language. I want
a beer behind the door marked NO TRESPASSING.

I mean to take every little bit of the good
advice any friendly yoyo wants to share
was what you said, and your dark wife weeps
while the liquored cat licks its dirty wounds.

When I rose up this morning I passed one man
I never saw who said it was a damn shame and I said
it was and no crap. Right there in the pouring
grit from Bethlehem's boiling stacks
that ate my own eyes, I said that

and said it again in the hanging city stink
while the sky came down like sheared tin over every
alky waking flopped and sick on the Pittsburgh asphalt,
and my boots said it all the way to the yard
where the forklift yammers in its teeth.

For years I've watched the corners for signs.
A hook, a jab, a feint, the peekaboo prayer of forearms,
anything for the opening, the rematch I go on dreaming.
What moves can say your life is saved?

    As I backpedaled in a field the wasp's nest waited,
    playing another game: a child is peeping out of
    my eyes now, confused by the madness of stinging,
    wave after wave rising as I tell my fists punish me,
    counter the pain. I take my own beating and God help

    me it hurts. Everything hurts, every punch
    jolts, rips my ears, my cheeks, my temples. Who hurts
    a man faster than himself? There was a wall to bounce
    on, better than ropes. I was eleven years old.

Eleven years ago I saw the fog
turn away and rise from the welts you were
to run away with its cousin the moon. They smacked
your chest and crossed your arms because you fell down
while the aisles filled with gorgeous women, high heels
pounding like Emille, the Champion, who planted his
good two feet and stuck, stuck, stuck, stuck
until your brain tied up your tongue and sighed.

    Somebody please, please, I cried,
    make them go away, but the ball in my hand had turned
    feverish with its crackling light. I could not let go
    as I broke against the wall. I was eleven years old.

Benny Paret, this night in a car ferrying
my load of darkness like a ring no one escapes,
I am bobbing and weaving in fog split only by a radio
whose harsh gargle is eleven years old, a voice in the air

telling the night you are down, counting time,
and I hear other voices from corners with bad moves say,
Get up, you son of a bitch, get up! But you will not
get up again in my life where the only sign you give me

is a moon I remember sailing down on your heart
and blood growing wings to fly up in your eyes.
And there, there the punches no one feels grow weak,
as the wall looms, break through the best prayer you had
to dump you dizzied and dreaming in the green grass.

Gray brick, ash, hand-bent railings, steps so big
it takes hours to mount them, polished oak
pews holding the slim hafts of sun, and one
splash of the *Pittsburgh Post-Gazette*. The man
who left Cumberland gone, come back, no job
anywhere. I come here alone, shaken
the way I came years ago to ride down
mountains in Big Daddy's cab. He was
the first set cold in the black meadow.

Six rows of track gleam, thinned, rippling
like water on walls where famous engines steam, half
submerged in frothing crowds with something
to celebrate and plenty to eat. One engineer takes
children for a free ride, a frolic
like an earthquake. Ash cakes their hair.
I am one of those who walked uphill
through flowers of soot to zing
scared to death into the world.

Now whole families afoot cruise South Cumberland
for something to do, no jobs, no money for bars,
the old stories cracked like wallets.

This time there's no fun in coming back. The second
death. My roundhouse uncle coughed his youth
into a gutter. His son, the third, slid on the ice,
losing his need to drink himself
stupidly dead. In this vaulted hall

I think of all the dirt poured down
from shovels and trains and empty pockets.
I stare into the huge malignant headlamps
circling the gray walls and catch a stuttered
glimpse of faces stunned like deer on a track,
children getting drunk, shiny as Depression apples.

Churning through the inner space of this godforsaken
wayside, I feel the ground try to upchuck and I dig
my fingers in my temples to bury a child
diced on a cowcatcher, a woman smelling
alkaline from washing out the soot.
Where I stood in that hopeless, hateful room
will not leave me. The scarf of smoke I saw
over a man's shoulder runs through me
like the sored Potomac River.

Grandfather, you ask why I don't visit you
now you have escaped the ticket-seller's cage
to fumble hooks and clean the Shakespeare reels.
What could we catch? I've been sitting in the pews
thinking about us a long time, long enough to see
a man can't live in jobless, friendless Cumberland
anymore. The soot owns even the fish.

I keep promising I'll come back, we'll get out,
you and me, like brothers, and I mean it.
A while ago a man with the look of a demented cousin
shuffled across this skittery floor and snatched up
the *Post-Gazette* and stuffed it in his coat
and nobody gave a damn because nobody cares
who comes or goes here or even who steals

what nobody wants: old news, photographs
of dead diesels behind chipped glass
swimming into Cumberland Station.

I'm the man who stole it and I wish you were
here to beat the hell out of me for it because
what you said a long time ago welts my face
and won't go away. I admit
it isn't mine even if it's nobody else's.
Anyway, that's all I catch this trip—bad
news. I can't catch my nephew's life, my uncle's,
Big Daddy's, yours, or the ash-haired kids'
who fell down to sleep here after the war.

Outside new families pick their way along tracks
you and I have walked home on many nights.
Every face on the walls goes on smiling,
and, Grandfather, I wish I had the guts
to tell you this is a place I hope
I never have to go through again.

There is no need of maps now, the interstate spooling
south of Roethke's country
gone sour: smokestacks thick as the risen fists of
robber barons, the burly smudge
of green he sang choked out by the Tonka Toy houses
the same mile after mile. Even snow
surprising in April can't soften Flint, the gray pall
Buick slides over Ann Arbor. Creeks
like steel rods in the buff ground make me think of fish
stiff in the neck to Toledo. Wind-
drift and grit surging through Ohio, toward Pittsburgh.
Night, the bored disc jockey,
cackling bad jokes to keep us awake: sequence of motions
through toll booths, more
bad jokes counting the miles of rain into Pennsylvania
spring. Changing stations, I
discover I've gone wrong above Altoona. It's too cold to be
where I should be at this hour.
At the truck stop the sleepy kid doesn't understand why
he's 100 miles wrong and I spin
the dial for any music, turning south once more until
Maryland welcomes me and the lustery
shield of Rt. 40 says Cumberland sleeps 37 miles west, its
cupped coal hills hugging
the family bones we walked away from for the sea. Is it
high black air that makes me shiver
or a room with an all-night light and a plant unwatered?
Above D.C. a truckstop, eggs, coffee,
one fat waitress greasy at the end of her shift, winking
to teamsters pale as a slug's belly. They

still hate long hair. For one dumb, instinctive instant
I touch the book in my hip pocket,
then sag and pay up. If only one would listen, I could
make Roethke ring and coo
all the hurts they haul in their grinding loneliness. I
still think I could do that
at 2 A.M. when the high beams flick up to discover the red
cardinal of Virginia. I can't
shake snow from my head and take the off-ramp five miles
from Fredericksburg. Between trucks, two
hours of sleep. Cramped as if tucked in a father's body,
I dream a room of starch
and ammonia, a woman clucking me off to bed, a man hating
for the last time the coal dust. Then
for no reason on earth light batters in from all sides,
fog like brainfire, stillness
awakes. And, as if I knew it would be, there on a grass
slope dogwood blooming. Reason
enough to shake deep when a truck backfires beyond trees
like a howitzer. The whole luscious
green world welcomes us. Why go on hurting ourselves with
ash sealing the rivers of Saginaw?
Why serve the executives of Buick who hate trout? Think
of the gray birds at Fredericksburg
gorging on our mothers' sons and Roethke in his green war
gone like Whitman, bulldozed
like the secret river of the soul, but not ended, only
diverted, carving new banks. Poetry,
who watches you easing out along a timber stand, as I do,
dreaming the feel of trunk bark,
cradling the insults we make to God? To wake up glad
by a field alive with more than words,
the dead singing our wars remembered and unremembered, is

to love your life and give it
a way to rejoice. Isn't home the same everywhere, the open
room of the sea, your hands
slippery with all the fish the fathers haul in their nets?
Damn death. Today I do not believe
a single sparrow will die but I will croak back his life.

PART 2

Somewhere on the side porch, in a viny haze of light,
you and I sift through pieces of a giant puzzle
to put together for once what must be
the Atlantic, a harbor unlikely
in the purest blue, a boat with a missing piece.

From a box of dark hand-rubbed hickory
music spools over our scratchy silence, the needle

sticks and when you flop back on the cool floor
I am gone into my white linen robe with stitches
of gold my mother made, constantly crossing herself.

The angelus cants in my mouth sometimes
like a tasteless wafer. Often I sing dreaming
what new puzzle my cash will buy

and later, missing notes because my voice cracks
over the open box I would never look into,
I break up in front of the puzzled faces of shifty
guards from St. Ignatius High, the same
bastards that took the all-city title
after spitting on our cheerleaders.

I take my cue from the other actor, his silence
after long speech I don't think anyone
truly hears. What did he mean
Render unto Caesar and the rest? I who am

the angel of song stand again in my wailing suit,
threadbare from years at the office,
cigarette burns, perhaps a little semen stain,

to make what one gaudy-cheeked woman said
was the road so many people needed
to find their way. In her foul breath
she hummed at my arm, croaking her thanks.

I didn't know any of those poor sons of bitches
who made me walk home thinking of a road out of town,
and I remember how once I broke down
sobbing harder than the great pipes.
They paid me double to hear me double their pain.

I only thought a girl was pregnant, whom I'd touched
wrongly and would die for, as the crow-footed nuns
flapped in their habits.

My voice was never half so good or pure as yours.
Probably you could, if asked, disinter each face,
recount how many points scored, where we lost
the piece with the head of the fisherman.

I've spent my whole life thinking we got screwed
by a maker of defective toys, learning
how not to hear my heart's
lonely knocked-up wheezing.

My God, how long does a man have to sing
to hear it be right just once, to ease out
some hope for the freckled kid whose
best give-and-go didn't make a diddly damn

though it beat me back to tears
long ago defeated as I croon at his wake?

Brother of the girl who needed no help from us
to conceive her own pains, my friend
today I sang maybe my last music
and bought a puzzle
of the entire charted world.

I promise even if I live to die
to get our colors in their right places, I won't
leave you alone under the vines until it's done,
until I sing like the most acute needle on earth
every note we dug out of those pressed grooves.

Sometimes I lie back down
in the morning
after I have splashed my face,
after eggs and cinnamon toast.
It is laziness, I know,
the act of a fool
who should do his work.
But I do it just the same.
In the cold I go to bed,
taking off only my boots,
and lay down my body
while the snow comes.
Sometimes like that
I do not believe the poems
I have written or read.
I hardly hear
anyone's language.
I lie with my chin
tight against my knees
and think of white fields,
how they stretch so easily
where I will never go.
I think also of the frosted
bones of a child resting
like me in a lazy drift,
waiting for someone to come,
to bend down and blow breath
like a happy, forgiving fog.
Sometimes I lie like that
all morning and whisper to
snow scratching the walls.

The girl was chosen at random. He pointed
for the mystical brunette behind her. As
in all crowds the distortions of distance
made her think he wanted her. So he did.
She was a ballerina, her toes were trained
to love grace and to spurn the simple boards
that in other guises were as high as any
worm might dream of rising. Her stability
had taught her to forget ideas, her heart
kept her floating like a fish's air sac.
She pumped and dreamed and pumped and held
for the long glide into sunset, just offstage.
But that afternoon coming down in midair
she felt she was near the nadir at last.
I think I'll go to a show she said to her
blonde hair. She wanted to feel life swirl
around the way a dying diabetic sneaks out
for cherry pie. The levitator comes in now
with his noisy, chattering finger. She rises
to the stage, to his hand, backstrokes in
the weeping willow fronds of her hair, sleeps.
We cannot see why or how it is done; deftly
his sword nicks her free, passes under breast,
buttock, thigh, and severs the dark cloud
between her gilded ankles and his slippers.
Then ideas fly back into her from every source,
ears, nose, mouth, and all the sly orifices,
until she gains back her weight and her sex.
The curtain closes and we all begin to cheer.
He will give her many children and great pain.

You climb in my arms and say
get me. I do,
I get you
with my face, my finger,
which wherever you are
turns to a rippling
laugh. On such days
I am more glad
than the mockingbird
with its mad mimic
for the rain that drives
you into my arms
like a broken wing.
I lift you up,
carry you from room to room.
I say somebody please
tell me what to do
with this gift.
I even pretend not to hear
you say how light
your body is in my grip.
I keep only the unspooling
laugh that sings
get me, and I do
with my nose, my mouth,
my one terrible finger
drawn across your heart
where breath goes on
like a gusting wind
and the rain is still
a room I can keep locked.

One day as the green grass sighed to the crow
I stepped onto shore's shoulder and left the sea
forever, and that is why sailors love me so.

Lanky and odd you may say I was, with hips slender,
a foreign accent, a gown like an antique dew.
I loved to dance. I had good teeth like a beaver.

How the girls groused and did go on is no secret.
I made their good men raise up from spring's tools,
with one glance I drew them to stuttered speech,

for there is no beauty such as mine. They poured
from rank hod and splintered hoe and hovel-tent.
My Lord, you are right to say I was devotedly wooed.

Night and day, by the scores I succored them.
I readily embraced their gods (which I do repent).
With a few of the weakest I may have lost my head

as in our gamboling we played the water's table.
But that, of course, was years ago. I was so new.
Shall I tell you how it was? Your poets fumbled

my fame so I hardly knew myself. A girl's head turns.
What wench they wished they chose and I became her.
I was the sheet spread for blessing a bride's bones,

or else I was the sun, too blinding to gaze upon.
Some sighed I was a cave. Some said I was the cry
of distress with tangled hair and legs unshaven.

I became the hacksaw blade, then the shackle's loop,
and when they came for me I was dark and shy and raw.
My circumstance was crude. What a girl must do,

she does, you understand. My seed thins, I droop.
Oh, I do not dance, I do not dance! I want a man,
the slap by firelight, that gusty two-fisted brute

crossing himself with claws. In hotels I sit and hum,
I have my moments. But the heroes I loved are gone.
Kiss and pity me now, I am the metaphor of bums.

One of them had a dental appointment, an abscess
having suddenly appeared, and when they kissed it was
the last kiss. Their mouths tasted of dead trout.
Daddy said, "Mommy, the dentist is a kindly sport
who likes to breathe death and rumor in his drill.
Why don't you go this very afternoon?" The dentist
had often told Mommy and Daddy how poison in the teeth
is a good surprise. Undetected, it attacks the body
like a horde of ravenous ants, he said. But the heart
is wise and bolts tight when it hears the ant-oars
splashing up the canals, he added. Naturally, he said,
this is a fine thing for business and it pleased him
to be able to do battle in such a wonderful cause.
Mommy said she wasn't sure what life was all about
but if he could remove the putrid trout, she'd come.
Daddy smiled and sent her off to the bus. The dentist
cocked her back in his dreamy chair, strapped her in,
and began to fill her with gas. But the poison stuck,
Mommy told Daddy, so she would require more time.
As the days passed she would sit under the dentist's
gaze and dream of her portable television, the menu
she must prepare for the Elks' annual dinner, and
she would sing little songs to remind her to pay
the insurance premiums. As each session ended,
the dentist would climb off her, remove and clean
his drill, and have the nurse suggest again the need
to brush thoroughly and constantly. Leave nothing Mommy,
nurse kept saying, and for God's sake think of yourself.
So Daddy came home from work, did the dishes, waited
for Mommy to get rid of her ants, and began to wonder

what life was all about. One day, summoning courage,
he asked Mommy how her teeth were. Mommy broke her
dinner plate on her forehead and said that's the last
time I eat dead trout. You go get your own dentist.

This is a poem about Nature. No use trying
to hide it. A woman in a bright blue Datsun
eased to a stop under a weeping willow tree
along state road five near Albany, Ohio. She
stood for a time near a brook brown with oil,
her hands folded across her swollen belly,
listening, as it seemed, to the elders' moans
at the edge of a field some distance south.
She conceived it to be a sigh of pleasure,
she was not dumb; somebody had got fucked.
But there was little time for such remorse.
Their church was not hers. She lay down,
the oil feeling like silk under her legs,
from which she had removed all clothing.
In a trice she delivered herself, the thing
slipping into her alabaster hands so quick
she did not look, but tried to nurse. Nothing.
This was the golden slipper no one could
wear, its back broken, smelling of long walks.
After awhile she threw it into the briars.
In the rearview mirror of the blue Datsun
she saw her ugly stepsisters waltz, shining
like angels in the aisles of jumbo jets. Out-
side of Albany she remembered that somewhere
the Toad was waiting to be kissed. Shifting,
she sang. She did not feel the thumps burst
beneath the baby blue machine that hummed,
hovered through the melon fields and summer.

Let us say you love a beautiful woman
whose obscurity you wish us to define.
Her name is Anyone, a petite child
who cannot sleep after sunrise.
She likes to hang her feet in rivers.
Tomorrow you will be married,
already the priest reaches
for vestments and homilies.
But tonight you hear in the wind
that Anyone is dead, raped, cut
from the cloth of your breathing
by the brother whose name is
in all your secondhand books.
After awhile a pesky salesman comes
to whisper about his goods: honor,
revenge, lies, and dull knives.
Until sunrise all you can think of
are unanswerable riddles, a game
to hide the mysterious ice in
Anyone's eyes. Later you hang
your feet in a river but it is
only wet and cold like the rain
sifting over you all night where
you have lain cool and quiet, barbed
on the hook at the end of a fine line.

She unzips her skirt, peels the nylons.
Her limbs are pale and smooth
as the back of a moving conch.
On this raw, conversational day
the crumpling articulation of her
underwear orchestrates her breath.
Beyond the window an impossibly
infinite vista spreads itself out.
The sea asserts all of its old reasons,
and contradicts, while you wait,
everything it tells you to trust.
Each single-minded water tuft
explodes its opposite as two terns
bank and tumble in an invisible wind.

At the corner of a field you remember,
your first girl lies down again,
those eyes staring up into the birch
that became a cage, her shy slender hands
easing back the plain cotton dress.
You stare at the lightning veins
of your wrist. Naked, tiny perturbations
of your cold skin will not go away
soon, disappear like any moment
that by the sea beats at your temples
like a madwoman's fists. You say that
now and know she doesn't care.

She doesn't want your life story
unless it leads to a new country.

Her tan is rich and warm. Cocked
against the window, her legs frame
sea light and her small-hair hangs
wild as grapevines. With her no one
will connect you to a good time.

If she has a name it is false.
As your tongue climbs her trunk,
what does it matter you can hear
fists of leaves beating down a street
swept by the sea? She rides you hard
and you forget to watch the boat
bobbing the horizon, dead in the water.
You love the shining sweat she wears.

Cynthia sits in the skimpy skin
of her brand-new nightgown,
her nakedness not subtle
as she recalls a dark angel
at the Queen City Drive-In,
which is where she has been,

and with him most of the night.
Had she wanted to watch movies
of Marlon Brando in fights?
Her angel kept hissing, "Honey!"
She kept sliding between sight
of denouements and appetites

she didn't know she had. Tough
to keep her balance she whispers,
thinking of "Buster, that's enough,"
though it wasn't by half.
She was saved by sudden trembles
of taillights and Brando's death.

Across the blazing lot plots
concluded in a rush, though
some calmly hung around.
Now Cynthia floats the town
in her gaze and exposes
something she should not,

some fresh thing discovered.
She sits like that for hours,
ignoring time and the motors
rooting the dark like lovers.
O angel, Cynthia's smeared
with joy and tiny flowers.

When I am drunk I may ask you to dance and give you
everything this life has given to me. Don't take it.
You will know who I am by the pine seed
in my nose, the mimosa fluting
all the way in the back where

there is also a '52 Chevy and the family I cannot find
in the photograph book which is all
I have left of my worldly goods.

Watch what I do with the casting forge: wheels, wheels,
pink ingots like babies spun from my hook, what they
taught me to do well before they kicked me out.
I know a man who said I could do it blind.
I believe that man said the god's truth.

Of all those I have fallen down with, I have died
for no one and do not want to die with Michigan
Avenue curbs to cuddle me. In my own life
I have cut down one who hung in a window

like a balding tire floating over the clay not far
from my lost Atlantic which has its own carcasses
to take care of. Chicago is a killer of drunks

who will kiss you for nothing, which is an angel's act.
I am no angel even blinded by the fury of wheels,
even sick for pines and cancerous women.
Just because I touch your coatsleeve
do you think I have nothing?

America, I worked my ass off for your piss-poor wine.
Sing to me now as you always claimed you would,
my life lies loose in my pocket like lint.

DOME POEM

Not, of course, the monster hunched downtown,
    with its rigid paws coiled into purchase
        where it seems to take a quiet shit,
    though it is certainly attractive enough,
with Parian marble and stained-glass slits,

to tell us something if we looked close instead
    of up, dizzying ourselves until we forget
        what it was we were looking at it for or
    where we are. But no, not that Whitmanian
lump of what is bigger and better than other

such creations. What we must have is so simple
    it constantly sits there like a shadow's
        shadow on water, bones and tendons slyly
    hidden so only the maker knows how it is
done, and it smiles and says simplify, simplify.

It is so much like America, too, that anyone
    inside looks out uninhibited on the stars
        which suddenly become real and intense
    like the rain beating wherever we are
until it is a waterfall of original innocence,

even though there may be a syphilitic finger
    gouging a tender trench. What matters to
        us is the words it can nourish, hold,
    even generate like scribes in slow sweat,
row on row distilling the King James that no

one of them thought more worthy than his poems.
      But a poem is a kind of country, full
            of tent stays and lines you always kick
      at night, politicians and old women with
old eyes loving the transparent, cheap silk

anybody can use to set up one of those lean-to
      lily pads. The good thing about a dome
            is the way the principle reduces, extends
      one drop of water to its proto-shape, one
wounded round atom smashing back in vengeance

it has never conceived in its watery head.
      Splitting the atom reveals the absence
            neither heart nor mind can bear, air,
      whose stout shell the dome leans on, that
darkness in and out of rooms, mouths, words.

He can only drink tea now, screwed and filed.
She is dead, in metal flecks.

55 years old and look like a bad nail
by God they yanked me out
I can tell you

soon as the hurt come son shut up
it don't mean nothing

but listen: you got time for a ride?

Habit's put the glass in his hands, the brown
tasteless tea, slime, and cigarettes.
Every Sunday the same old dog
fat at his feet.

Ain't so much me I'm asking for
dog like to get out and piss
thinks they remember.

Near the main gate of Gary Steel I stop.
The amber light pours out of stacked horizons,
monstrous cranes hang over suburbs.

She thinks that piss mean something
it don't mean nothing.

Turning back in the dark, headlights flash
on our faces, bent, light of a woman's hair.

I

Don't women, Mr. Ransom, as much as geese
deserve a voice? Must we be tasked
with silence, be always the antecedents
of your pedantic? What is the purpose?

> *Think twice,*
> *madam, then speak as befits*
> *your station. I control myself in masks,*
> *in loving birds, as Apollo did.*
> *All surface consists of hide and grease.*

Benign heart, your intelligence chafes
my passion and leaves it sharper.
It's possible you are wrong
to beget me with force
and nothing to say.
I want a divorce
from undainty birds that wander
through no time. My tongue
wants words hotter than you made.

> *Nothing sears*
> *but fails; chills are the rule.*

Yet early and late, must I be lost?
Why did you make plot with weather?
Why did you give old Conrad new tools

to heckle me in rhyme and meter,
to shake his fist at space?
I waited while,
disobedient, he jeered.

Fear.

2

Yes. Yours in Conrad's fist.
Grief as of a hung face
that the sweating soldier mistook
for nerves' tick, no worse,
so turned vaguely tired home.
Walking thus, suddenly afraid
of done and undone, he looked
for a shop to get drunk. Spades
already echoed on the road
where they rolled the rock.
Always whores, we were dismissed.

Back at the argument (I think
you might say, though not in lines)
              those Greek birds wink.
Conrad knew this. His belief in art's
exclusion I granted . . . is there time? . . .
to enforce the love I knew to be
our sequel, you. In what they are
these birds say the only story.
Conrad agrees, for I have asked him:
in verse a woman must depart
yet remain, essence of everything.

This is medieval stuff and indicts
my husband and my maker, but at last
I am the one who cries in goose and grief,
gardened with loss and no relief.
I give you words with artifice
that never could break ice.
You gave me this empty face,
Conrad's wife's. I wanted more.
Now I give it back as you go forth
from widow's arms, parsing crowns
of stars, unbent, puzzling device.

I do not believe in Madame Margo's palm.
There is no earth smelling of rotted plums
between her thumb and the jeweled fingers.
This death she speaks of is a cheap one.
We all die. It is nothing to say that.
So that time when the others drank wine
on the way to her tent, I remained
alone by the bumping river, happy, light
from the fire telling me its true story
as the waterbugs skidded in chaos and fear.
Last night I dreamed of you once more.
I know what even Madame Margo does not know
and when I climb the hill for more wood
I find you are dancing away in little clouds
my breath makes. Do not be afraid of her,
do not think of this death she awards you.
I ask you, did you say look into the candle?
In the dream I saw you doing two things.
First you were sitting at a fire, then
you tried to find the waterbugs under rocks.
When you discover you are growing cold
you must immediately come to me. I will
tell you why your fingers are all naked.

To Mary Alice Cornwell

1. Churchland Summer

That cemetery in the place hallowed by
its name, cramped like all cemeteries in the East,
overburied, overburdened ground, groaning with
deadly replicas of unlikely angels,

I have been back there in the stubbed wilting grass
burned brown as locusts on the oak's trunk,
but not often and never in winter
in the pulse of snow-whirl, and maybe
cold is not the season I have
to pack in and go for the feeling of what
comes to me all this blustery day, your hand
like the sea enormously cool in my fever. O that,

but not only that, the ur-anguish, I have no word for.

Maybe in heat, with dust sinuous on the dirt roads,
dust grained and deep in the seat of my pants,
on my face like ashes.

I have cozened you from the roots of gardens,
found you in dim rooms down on your broad back.
I was out of breath, too, afraid to move.

There was plenty of dirt on that day, and heat,
yet I did lean late after midnight to whistle
an old song over the chair where the wool you

wove knotted what warmth
a dying woman can keep in her breath,
and you were cold. I am as sure it was so
as the season you called Black August.

Who is accused in this? Not that grass
parched, ticking where I came to stand in

the glib knock of the dirt where they pressed you
dry as a bulb while the cicadas wailed. Does anyone
with red eyes and stunned tongue understand this?

I don't care that you died, I want to keep alive
the love you made good in me. So who can tell me

how to stop dreaming those bones charred by cold,
the frame of the stripped skin,
the real absence of eyeholes?

2. Back River Winter

For some good time I mourned you only in walking
through heat-haze and the fat proud wildflowers
where the fireflies waited for us to run.

But in winter which is infinitely young
with a rumpled white sheet that invites all
cessation to the tumbling pain in the nerves?

There are apples in the yard, red and soft.
Who would ask why they fell? What they say, buried
in their dark skins, their seeds more perfect than reason,

is less inaudible than weeping. I have some need
to speak of final things in my own tongue, perimeters
I must keep to like the cautious wheeling fishhawk

who eats the apples in bad times. Today in snow
I watched them peel a man from his tree-clenched car.
I saw the wrecker slide with its prize, go away

like a fat woman, like you, a kind of jolly dance
turned sour that with one finger I could blot out.
Then was gone. Was snow. Was mud bridging its wound

and not even a bluejay to break that vision. Yet
I did walk out by the river cheerfully feathering
the same sun I could pretend was my daughter's hair

and in pines knotting up odd shadows, believe it
or not, I could imagine I heard the promised Christ
beautifully breathing that dead man's name.

Tonight someone in the cold will ask as I ask
what is the trick of it? In this weather I think
I must learn how to walk out of despair, to see

what the apples fall into is a place without answer
or asking, and accept it as the fishhawk does, the man
who drives the wrecker and sings a song of one

woman he has not loved for the whole of a single night.
I must give over grief and begin in the winter
I love to love whatever believes in the good.

And if you should find me whistling your old fame
among great-grandchildren, remember it is what
you have taught me, and nothing less will I know.

When it stopped the sun suddenly poured through
the thorned black locusts and that boiling
slopped over those branches, quicksilvered
across the new lacy surf of the lawn,
rose up beyond the windowsill,
frothed against the glass
until I would let it in,
and though I huggered
at my abstract hurt
no thorns

I could feel snagged in any metaphysics
I spread out. I can tell you I was
unprepared for the swelling
your arms made at my neck
like a whispered joy.
Then I had to let out
the dog, turn off the TV,
give up my good excuse
to go on writing
hard things

and it was just then the children came
swaddled up like small pines, glittery,
speckled for their own celebrations,
their eyes pumping up
what was left of my heart,
so we went out for hotdogs,
and went all night on our
bellies under the black

locusts, until you
fell with me, soggy
in bed, in love,
in the dark.

THE SPRING POEM

Everyone should write a spring poem.
—Louise Glück

Yes, but we must be sure of verities
such as proper heat and adequate form.
That's what poets are for, is my theory.
This then is a spring poem. A car warms
its rusting hulk in a meadow; weeds slog
up its flanks in martial weather. April
or late March is our month. There is a fog
of spunky mildew and sweaty tufts spill
from the damp rump of a backseat. A spring
thrusts one gleaming tip out, a brilliant tooth
uncoiling from winter's tension, a ring
of insects along, working out the Truth.
Each year this car, melting around that spring,
hears nails trench from boards and every squeak sing.

The ladder quakes and sways under me, old wood
I put too much faith in, like ancestors strained.
You circle me, cradling the baby, sun guttering
in your face, parading through the leaves, glad.
If I looked down I would see your calm fear, see
in your narrowed eyes my bones chipped, useless.
The bucket hangs from my belt, pulling obscenely
at my pants, but the cherries drop in and grow
one by one. I keep reaching higher than I need
because I want the one that tickles your tongue.
When I come down we will both be older, slower,
but what of that? Haven't we loved this climbing?
If the ladder gives way I still believe I can
catch one branch, drop the bucket and ease down.

DRUNKS

A poetry reading at the V.A. Hospital for the Rehabilitation of Addicts and Alcoholics, Battle Creek, Michigan

I.

Nobody on the lawns, the impeccable fairways.

That's what you drive through here.
                    Oh, maybe one man
pulls a golf cart. No clubs in his bag.
They do not allow clubs. He plays
in his head, smack, flight, and the gliding game.
                    Nobody with him,
nobody to say, *Hey Buddy, watch your damn ball;* or,
          Jesus, you blew it again.

Driving, you watch him shrink in your rearview
mirror. Alone. Keepers stay inside, warm, smart.
They watch. No clubs are allowed.

2.

          Buildings hunch ahead ringed in shrub,
harsh evergreen. Snow domes that sad brick, windows
wear yellow even lids. Big doors grip like molars.
                    Grass ripples
so clean it seems unreal, dark as the swept shoulders
of businessmen who never tip the bootblacks because
          they smell like bad wine or dirt.
Nobody moves.
                    No scraps, no letter fading, crumpled

74

at a curb, no cigarette wrapper hustles. You blow
stale breath on fingers suddenly cold, read numbers,

move on more afraid than you were. What do they want?
        You say an uncle's name, one who was
            fat, pink, and dead drunk.

3.

Past blighted elms, ragged pines, sharp winter sun
warms in their hands where they wait for you, anonymous
faces tight in that just-got-up cold splash.
                            You drift around
curves, sink back toward the uncle, Biggie, his hand
    reaching for the bottle, the knife still
        whispering over your head, that flash as it

stabs the wall, missing you, missing the woman, but
    still hurting years after moss pressed its rag
        cold on Biggie's shattered veins. You track
            the limb-shadows and remember flat-bellied

college girls, good tans, skirts like mimosas, long ago.

4.

You don't expect the thin Negro who bolts across the lawn
shirtless. It's below freezing. You nose the car into space
marked RESERVED. The man who comes out, a counselor,

says it is nobody, nobody. He leads you through wire cages,
past Coke and candy machines. The lights say empty, try
somewhere else. There, hands jammed in torn pockets, they
fall in behind you, their footsteps, yours, one sound.

If you asked who died someone would step out, step, then
turn away. One man crosses lawns like a shot gazelle,
his black woolly hair leaping.

5.

The counselor says you're the freak, rich writer.
He walks so keys jingle loudly on his belt.
At the front of the room,
suddenly alone, you crack a window. Their eyes run over you
cold open. They could stone you if one drunk
screamed, *Get him!* Nobody says a word.

You gulp cold coffee they bring, grin to the hands holding
wooden ashtrays, tables that jerk
uncontrollably.

Biggie's nails always split
down the middle in the cold. Bad lumber, he whined, but
he couldn't hit straight. The hammer's half-moons
bloomed on his bones and his palms got used
to coiling like claws.
You open the book of poems.

6.

Wind seeps at your back but you sweat, watch white hair
like the crown feathers of zoo birds, pheasants maybe,
rise and drift and fall. It would be easy to see a single man
break down and beg on a street corner, but not so many
as these. How many corners would it take?
They welcome you
because you come from the world with a corner for each one.

Only the poem dies
and will not lie happily in the gutter. You make
a curse like a cop's in their ears. Among
soldiers you confuse the drab greens
of this room with day rooms, ward rooms,
jail-green drunk tanks. Wind seeps.
When they laugh you want to buy them all drinks.
Instead you make bad jokes about hating
armies, about getting out one day.

                              Nobody laughs.
Nobody laughs.
            You push the window wider. No black gazelle,
only shrub grinding the brick. From here nobody can see
the golf course, the clubless player you admire
so casually. *They'll catch him downtown.* Why? *That's where
we go when we can. No place else to go.* No money.
No credit. They don't deliver here.

7.

Hey Bud them poems make you any money?
They drum their fingers, big high school rings, smoke, drink
coffee. They make you see they know what counts,
why you came here, writer, freak, but
make it easy, as if you were family
come home, made good, with poems full of money,
old street corners, cheap whiskey.

8.

You begin again. One in the back leans out
of an unstable dream, pokes his gray head behind a table
                              (Biggie's playing scary games

the neighbor's girl screamed.)
and tumbles, a whiskery heap. You whisper, "Get up easy."
He laughs first, the drunk's con, be funny,
throw loud pies in your face for a drink; when laughs

dribble off like spittle, his eyes dry grim,
deep as corks slapped back in the bottleneck
too many times. Your voice warps like a struck saw

through bar poems that say you want to take them home
to the sweet greasy lights of taverns, cut
back to smoke that holds the friend in pain,
the war buddy, the dead guy that owes you.

No money, no dice, no roll. You
pour poems over the room like dollars
burned, like the soft hips of women swaggering
with plates of beer in those flush, early hours.

Nobody laughs.

9.

Biggie couldn't read or write. He played Jew's harp.

One fat man in a polo shirt
three rows back puts his hand on his hip
and stands up mean as a beat walker, the hurt
on his forehead a thick red scar. He's quick
with hate. But words won't come first,
only fists. Then a torrent, curses
he's never said, shiny slugs. *Prick,*
he screams, *You're nobody. Who's worse*

than you are? You come out here to get rich
on us. What do you care about drunks? A girl
you hadn't seen appears beside him,
touches his arm, sits him down, whirls,
and disappears. You quiver, stick
cigarettes in your mouth. Hurt,
you wonder why you came. Sick,
you stumble through poems like closed doors.

10.

Three men break for coffee, cards in the room by the Cokes.
Later, when you leave, they laugh.

Bumming cash and cigarettes paid Biggie back. His shoe
split with a secret passage: *Boy that's for one
bottle for when I go.* Five bucks.

They'd never find it no matter how much they beat him.
They beat him dead,
dumped him on the porch. Neighbors passed that
night. Drunk, they said. Stupid, drunk.
We said he was drunk again.

They like your story.
Something between you now. Is that what they want?

11.

Fictions. Drunk uncles left for dead.
Scorn, loneliness, shame, pummeled brains, split
hands. What's left?
Butchered ambition, pawn tickets, old pictures

in wallets moldering like corpses. Hang on, hang on
to alleys, flush pimps, cold-water whores, both shoes.
They want anything to take back to the rooms where
you have to dream to stay alive: poems

        must smell like cash, stick like Coke to the skin,
        wear shedding coats, get the shakes, throw up
        on wives still loved, sing country and western

fictions. You read Hemingway's "Killers."
They know the world a battered boxer knows.
Ole Anderson makes them quake like hooked meat.
                            They understand killers
from the feet up. Ankle coats, suits full of holes.

You stop when the motorman enters the café: what now?

You make them writers, claim anybody
could come in that door, anybody, whatever they want.
They laugh, nobody fooled. Magically, they reach
for guns, turn ashtrays to sawed-off carbines.

Blow the mother's brains out!   Not anybody,

they know who's coming in. The fat one shouts: *Killers
don't come for no reason. Anderson had it coming.*

Bad break. Bad break.   Nobody says that.

12.

       Fictions. The room is dizzy with sheer breath. Alleys
open now, somebody on the run, puking from the heart.
You go back to the poems.
                    On the sofa you fake sleep. Your aunt
                    follows Biggie out back, his rich shoe
                    dragging. *What do they want Biggie?*

13.

The next time you see Biggie dead drunk, dead.
Fictions. The counselor says
what you saw was nobody, nobody. That shadow runner
no shot gazelle, nobody.
                You try to catch him
with poems for black angels, drunk angels, but too late.

They leave silent, in twos, threes: KP, toilets,
facts the boozeless need to live. Bad news.
One comes up alone, hands shy behind him. Does he know
who Ole Anderson ran from, or where Biggie went? You planned
to tell him thank you, but Anderson got away.
                      Would he believe it? No.
He's tall black. Green jungle fatigues, sunglasses
hide him like a secret in a rented room. He turns your hand
in the brother's grip, wants your name
on the torn flat of a buck pack.

                      Fictions.
You line it out in red.   Ask the angel's name,
he says, you'll find him sometime.

14.

        You drive out slowly, sweat-sodden, chilled so deep
you think no laughing drunk can ever make you warm again.
                          Odd black squirrels shoot down
      the elms, cross blind, gambling you'll stop and look.
      At the last corner there's a sign for traffic
      nobody remembers. Fairways are empty everywhere.

The counselor said few graduate for good. Graduate from
what you asked, but you were done and so was he.

15.

At every bar you pass you slow but see no sleek gazelle
face down like a man lining up a putt. Killers,
bristling silverfish rustle in your hair,
go nowhere but home to Biggie, singing on his porch,
his breath sweet vomit, his shoes rich and cold.

Somehow you know the corner where the angel is
and halfway home you stop and learn to say
the only name you ever knew, and find him
waiting alone, tears fat on the back of his hand,
crazy drunk, waving at the gaudy world like family.

PART 3

The sun frets, a fat wafer falling like a trap of failed mesh.
I watch the pin-glare of a mockingbird's eye cut sharply, descend
on the blank water, then emerge from himself naked
as a girl who shimmered here, once, for me.

If we come back like penitents to kneel over water, bass swirling,
scattering the mayflies that often, in silence, graze

lips, what is the word floating out from the mouth unbearable
as a bird's black grin or a madman's lust?

The word is not *we* but *me*. Giving it again and again

brings no one out of the willows and I, willing to believe
like a sap in whatever dives or rises, hear no voice
but the mist sizzling on stones. I lift my head

for echoes out of trees, for the flashed recoil of flesh hung
cheap and gaudy, wingless, above the stab of water
that crunched her like a beer can. Toads honk

the only answer. Among them, a boy, I felt

the grotesque pull of the moon all night, peeled and went slowly
down in terror, rising, falling through the pulpy leaves
until the sun caught me, drained, and I was no one
wanted, so walked away from all knowing,

walked into town and drank, calmly, an illegal beer, then slept.

The hooks, in hairy hands, clawed it smooth as a dish, a super-
human search by flood-and-firelight. What could they find?
Like many, I have been out of town a long time.

I wish the face floating above the chill at my knees opened
the door of a drab hotel. I wish it said, *Go to hell,*
or *Do you know what time it is,* anything

that, if I heard it, I could kneel to and swear to be faithful.

Tonight no one takes fish. Tattered pennants
of T-shirts flap, their shadows riding wave crests,
among the hulls half-ashore and wholly sunken.
Always I am the waterman snagging nets on keels
in the graveyard of boats, the pale sailor who
glides with the music of nails through plank rot
and oil scum to sit in the toy wheelhouse of fathers.

I do not ask you to come with me or even to watch
the pennants signaling the drift of the winds.
Nothing I could do would raise one body bound
under these mud-struck beams, but I mean to do
what I can to save my own waterlogged life and here
is the best place I know to beg. I throw out love
like an anchor and wait where the long house lights
of strangers tickle the river's back. I go alone

as a creaky-boned woman goes to the far bench
at the heart of her garden where the rose suffers.
There will be time for you to hold in your palm
what each has held here, the sudden canting of gulls,
a room with one back-broken chair, the potbelly
sputtering as it answers the wind, the soft knock
waters make at the fair skin of roots. I come here
to stop up my lying words: your life was always bad.

Isn't it right to drag the rivers for the bodies
not even the nets could catch? I won't lie, I want
you to lie with me on the tumbling surface of love.
This is the place to honor crab song, reed's aria,

where every hour the mussel sighs, *Begin again.* Say
I am water and learn what I hold as river, creek,
lake, ditch, or sewer. I am equal with fire and ice.
We are one body sailing or nothing. My life, yours,
what are they but hulls homing, moving the sand?

The babies from Cumberland are dying, mister.
You know the question that everybody asks
over the oysters, the crabs, the whiskey:

after all these years, and you making good cash,
why for Christ's sake have you turned up now?
What kind of answer can you hang on that?

I think of blue hydrangeas, a woman's form,
the river they are all going to die by soon
if they survive small defeats in the shipyard.

Where are the answers to all the questions
not asked? I come back mumbling at death,
cursing church, lilies, and no resurrection

strong as the spring tides that know how to lift
when they want any lover's good-looking girl
who was buried by pines in her fever and fits.

I should have been one kneeling in boots and boats
but she made me leave the stink of baitshacks,
the teeth of clam rakes harping the old bones.

The babies from Cumberland got winded, people.
I drink in her house that once was so upright
and repent one crazy Christmas when the three

cons and I stole cheap wine then kissed her
into sleep. She said she dreamed the Mallard
none of us could knock down with that .22 pistol.

How answer now her old lies, her waddling gait
when they hurt me? I swear I'm not loving you
bastards anymore, even if you die in her wake.

I say that for her to an assembly of worms
and the sexton slips in with a shovel to split
the marsh for Cumberland's baby come to term.

Aubrey Bodine's crosswater shot of Menchville,
Virginia: a little dream composing a little water,
specifically, the Deep Creek flank of the Warwick.
Two-man oyster scows lie shoulder to shoulder,
as if you walk them, one land to another,
no narrow channel hidden in the glossy middle
like a blurred stroke, current grinning at hulls.
It is an entirely eloquent peace, with lolling
ropes and liquid glitter, this vision of traffic
and no oystermen in sight. Clearly, Bodine is not
Matthew Brady catching the trenchant gropes frozen
at Fredericksburg with a small black box. So well
has he excluded the neat Mennonite church, yachts,
country club pool, the spare smell of dignity seeps.
Perhaps it is because of the zoom on the teeth
of the oyster tongs; perhaps it is after all Sunday.

Above the last boat, the flat-faced store squats
at the end of the dirt road as if musing over
accounts receivable. No doubt it has weathered
years of blood spilling. A spotted hound lifts
his nose above what must be yesterday's trash fish,
his white coat luminous against deep foliage. What
Bodine fails to see is the dog turning to lope
uphill under that screen of poplars, behind fat
azaleas that hide the county farm and the drunks
pressed against wire screens, sniffing the James.
One oysterman thumped his noisy wife (the window
was accidental) because she had a knife and mourned
their boy twenty years drowned. If he knew Bodine

stood at the marsh tip where his boy dove, if he
were but told a camera yawned to suck in the years
of his worst sailing shame, he would turn away. He
would whistle up boys in the dust that is dignity
and if he could he would spit in his hand and tell
his nameless black cellmate there are many men
for whom the world is neither oyster nor pearl.

Flecks of dust black as pepper in the tricky sun
that, at the ridge, deflects from pines

leaves the little creek you go down to dull,
gray as its grated bottom. No green
word describes what floats
there, a kind of spinach,

tatters of the heart, infinitely soft because
this is one of those places the light
moves through like a monk,
obsequious, everything

the numinous reminder of how what lives leans
with currents, out of the dark, wants
to burst the cowl of habit

become blossom, but could not, would dry out
exposed, and drift, stiffened,
like music badly remembered.

Patria mea est rises as you kneel for a close look;
faces, a girl and a woman, skid like waterbugs,
flakes you cannot hold

like the blown flags under water. One
word, missing, nags you up the cold stone

where light cracks like the cooling tractor.
It follows you into the kitchen, across linoleum
worn like marble, hangs

with the dying vine in the window. You cradle
the coffee and the bread, then predict rain.
The woman, brittle as the earth,

gives you her back, biting it off. "Good."

There is something else. Once I woke up in the bed
of a farmer's hog-dungy truck because in a bar
I said I hoped I would die in the lick of the James
and he said, "I taken you home for the reason
who'd know but you was dumb enough to do just that?"

Most people don't believe there are men keeping sisters
prowling their attics. He was one.
What I know about wanting not to go nuts, about how
to love my own simple life, I take from two
whose speech came like windows scraping.

Mostly she was locked up good and he would talk
as we wandered up the tiny stairs and walked
through the gallery of girls she sketched
on sheets and tacked to the eaves. He shook
his head for the purity of what she made, although
she dreamed plain: each girl wore green, as she did,

the rent streak of the crayon blurring into the hubs
of spinning wheels always there, and legs skewed out
like bad-cut boards and faces facing to a window
hardly more than a butter smear. Two weeks
I heard him whisper through the hole in his throat

the neighbors must not know or else they'd think
being crazy's just the joke the artist plays.
As serious as if he'd laid a knife on a hog's throat
he swore that art was the only thing that mattered

in this moony world. *You saw it? Didn't you see it!*
Upstairs she thumped her boards and drooled.

Maybe like him I would want to die for art's cash.
He said that, too. He was wrong.
What good is the passion that keeps a woman
croaking for a man with more than one screw loose
and lines her life with infinite angles of pain?

When I left he warned me to keep away from the James
and I have done the best I can in a hundred towns
where no one took me home to keep me living. You
would be wrong to think I do not love
the way that woman soared in shades of green.

Maybe some destroyer way out sent the wave,
the sea will carry such news without a man's asking,
maybe the net was too heavy and I slipped.
It could have been that, by God.

I don't know what it was. I was alive
and the sun hung on my face like a bruise one day
in 1945 when no Japanese gave up on a black island
that wasn't my own Egg Island Bar but
could have been the way it knocked me out.

What it is is a hole you can't even see. I do not want
to talk about this rupture or why the wife
of my two boys who was once thin as a bowline
has begun to stink like a rotting hawser.
We are like Diggs's funeral advertisement,
EVER FAITHFUL TO ONE HIGH STANDARD.

Both boys came home in a box. You could put your fist
in the holes they wore and she has been a little
nervous ever since. Why shouldn't she
hold something back? What's
the meaning of waste, anyway?

I'll tell you what I know. The smell of salt is good
but the sea is nobody's friend. I don't know
what my boys smell like now but I see
the two of them stuffing their shirts
way up in the wedge of the bow,
after clams and I don't know what all.

I don't have the words to say this out plain, forgive me.

I was alive and then I was hurt and then I was dead
and then I was alive, that's how it was.
I see her drying the boys but I don't
see the wave coming which was when
the last thing I heard was a gull.

If you woke up staring into a scaled, stinking pile
of shirts not worth a good damn, the sun
boiling out of your life, hurt so bad
you don't know how to get home,
wouldn't you wonder why?

I cut my nets loose, I drifted, I said to no one
Jesus, what rotten thing have I done now?

Somewhere behind me the clank and jerk of a crane clears houses,
echoing like weightlifters in bare rooms. Water fills
basements where families once muscled like schools
of fish. The yachts bob in neat lines, gleaming

in the big plate-glass window of the new country club. Gulls peck
a meal from the disgorged mud. I hear the squeege of black
tires taking the buffets of water,

protecting the white, pure flanks. Later, there is the cross
of a sailboat's mast and, underwater, the moons
of portholes bulged eerily

like crab eyes. Crabs can't see. They live by smelling
the rotten hunk of a chicken's neck. I toss it out like a bribe,
careful to make no sudden noise, cast no shadow.

They have arms like Samson and I, only ten, know that pull
from the water has to go through fingertips transmitting
the stretch and tear of flesh without sound or shape
and will be what it means to stand staring
in the sun, hungering for yachts.

It means waiting while cranes smash your house. Waiting.

Where I have come from, why, does not reveal itself anymore
until the sun burns me back to three black children,
older and larger, who will beat my ass again

in this memory, who will bebop something I don't know how to say.
Listen, the mud clots my eyes. Bleeding, I watch them
scramble uphill through gulls, the slide
I know only in scream already started.

When I go home someone will ask what has turned me black all over.

I cannot give them crabs or answer anything for years.
They will whip me again.

All night I dream of big arms jerking chunks of white meat, black
dreams filling my room with wheeze and bang, my hand paying
out the crab line that breaks for the last time.

Two black children are crying like gulls, mud-skinned like me,
for one whose eyes bump blindly at the moons of the white
hull where the long-armed mast sways. I wish I could
tell them my father will come and save the one

who for a joke stole all I ever caught before the mud
gave way and the sun, shining on his hand,
sank,

but I am only ten,
too small to climb the crane where my father grins.

Am I at home here, humpback nub,
             nub of nothing, rock where pines
preen in wimpling winds,
             roots with capillaries bulged,
sucking seamist to live? I oar out
             anyway, wallow through troughs,
go where brothers, fathers lie
             and won't speak, dreaming, too, and
landing, lug the rowboat oafishly
             onto an island I can circle three
times each hour, barely running,
             reeds, muck-suck oozing my feet,
the only one today to love these
             lovely hulls. Yet how at home
where nobody lives? Who is the one
             whose body I row through the sun?
When I set out I meant to fish
             on the clean beach, cast with killdeer
going insane in that pas de deux
             the black waves banter, under-
cutting the stage they tick on. But
             I have no rod, am no fisherman in this
bronze October light. Scrambling from
             deck to deck, on the shells of dead
fishermen's boats, I feel the families
             pulling back alive while tides bubble
through stoved-in sterns. Silence
             in this junkyard of currents rots,
reeks, absorbs bleached carcasses of
             trout, jellyfish, lung-busted oysters,

seagoing bugeyes with impeccable
                    equality. The elements are everywhere
rising, meager flecks of flesh decomposing
                    on spears of wood, glittery chips
wedged like gold in the ventricles of weed.
                    I run. I came here not to be alone,
to belly-flop, tripped forward on my face,
                    running blindly, as if to catch
some image of myself, some clown I greet
                    in a shard of windshield, whose big
feet I keep running into. Today, balance
                    snatched by a fool's tide in my head,
I caught my toes, stuck, hooked in the rot-
                    blossoming head a confused grandfatherly
turtle eased out in the wrong place
                    at the wrong time. Cartwheeling, flying
backward into his blood-rush, my mouth gives
                    its kiss to a reed-beard. I tumble
into holes where deep-set irises blinked
                    against huge buffetings of cold steel
flukes that might have been a killer
                    whale's. I breathe that stale, distant
death not quite relinquished from an island
                    floater hollowed by the brass wheel
of homebound oyster scows. That's what
                    it means to come up dumbly wrong, fixed
in the deceptive cocksure self's notion
                    of navigation. A being empties all over
again heart, fish-stuffed gut, still
                    threshing bones, its jaw snapping nothing
where I lay full-length as Gulliver. Sun
                    bleeds through the rear slope of his
house, warming sand crabs who come waving

one weak claw, gropers digging their
wind-beaten, juice-stewing bodies, tiny
            silhouettes making cave shadows against
what weirdly transforms from heroic swimmer
            to storm-proof charnel house for crabs.
And who lives here? Who gets up in that
            simple click of survivors, skin sored
with fresh blood, and holding a nose, goes
            to the lock-rattling boat at the island's
edge?
            Most days I leave with no answer
            I did not always have, let tide pull take
the channel to the pulsed light in a widow's
            window, and row until the salt crescents
my cheeks. By night silver squibs, Spanish
            mackerels, dance in the air as if dredged
from dreams. Unseen, they plummet dead-
            pan like old jokes on darkened stoops.
Tonight, halfway across, my arms sag, oars
            drift and tell of thunderstruck turtles
turned senseless in their wakes. It is
            the dead calm of tide turn that possesses
me to leap up, straddle the seat planks,
            rock until I thump out a swell of paddle
percussion for the half-headless, wholly
            homeless floaters stunned on course, and
becoming what they never thought of—
            what the ghostly radar of crabs homes at,
claims, turns to a new temple, enters,
            claws high, no grief, no joy imagined.
In darkness, I slap a tune for dark ones
            who eat and breed and age in hoods
they surrender to the meat of the living.

Rounding a slip of the marsh, the boat skids
under me and the propeller whines naked,
then digs and shoots me forward. A clapper rail
disappears in reeds and one crane, shaken
from his nap, blinks and holds.

He makes me think of the Lost Tribe of Virginia,
as if the scree of insects were the Jew's
harp in John Jacob Niles's mouth.

A creek opens its throat and I enter, dragging
down to hear my wake's slip-slop,
thinking of the man who warned me people
were the same everywhere, lost and wondering

how they came to the life no one else wanted.
Sweet Jesus, he was right. Now he lies
in this sodden ground for the first time
in his life and I do not know even where.

Today is no different, the waters flood hulks
of empty houses, leaving beer cans to gleam
in the indifferent moon. The first stalks of
narcissus break the ground with gold
though March still means tonight to freeze.

I know this place, its small mustering of facts
wind-worn and useless, real and repeated, the same
anywhere. At the end the creek leads to a room,
one placid boat swinging at a stick, pines sieving

air, the cleat ringing like small jewelry.

You need to know these boats, cunners, square
of bow and stern, never painted, always with a bottle
floating where the bilge is always rank and deep.
Sometimes they hold the sun like a butter tub but
nobody ever stepped a sail in one. They're used
to ferry out to where the oyster scows squat, sere
and long as a lovely woman's thigh in an old dream.
You need to ask why they lie cracked, sucking salt-
water through the reed tubes, what has happened
to shove them back into the center of the marsh
where the scree of gnats goes out when a fisherman,
desperate in the end, shoves his finger in his ear.
You need to hear the slow toll of rope ends, mossed
like drifting arms, the bell-cry of cleat and chained
transom stained a hundred hues by the licking sea.

When the dozers come to take the marsh, slapping down
layers of asphalt, when the all-temperature malls and
the good women of the garden club cease designing,
they will be gone, claimed by antique freaks, smashed
for scrap, the creeks leveled, the sun deceived with
only steel to flash on in the heat. They're unemployed,
no swimming boys will sink them for a joke, no wind
whip and toss them in a storm or leave them in a tree.
The fishermen exchange their good hard poverty for jobs
behind counters; few men ever rowed a boat on dirt and
what you'd get for one is not enough for one week's beer.
It is for this, because you need to know, I give you
the last cunner of all, its charred bottom still whole,
crabs and other creatures not yet gone, a man's hat
floating in the black water as if mislaid, going down.

WHAT THE WATERMAN PRAYED

For John Haislip

I never asked for money, that's one thing.
I asked to see some good, a simpleton's act
of sense in all his sins. I never asked not
to die, only for grace to do it right. Who
asks for the woman that makes a man whole?
She gave me eight children in the same bed,
two girls who sank the boats I carved in love.
When both married bad I never asked for help
they couldn't give themselves. We live
in rooms whose shades are cracked by time.
I, being of sound mind, hope none of us die
until tomorrow or next week. Hope is not
prayer, which is all the truth I know.
I've been down on my knees, up to my ass
in knees, but my two girls died. I did not.
It wasn't prayer that helped me fail
the lives I've held. The roar in my head
tolls wind over water, a way of talking
to that rolling dark where I learned
what judgment is. It means casting nets
in depths great enough to lose your fear
when something's deeper yet to lose. Sons
will always pray not to hear I'm drunk again,
Job come home with his bewildered heart.
Men learn the things they can't pray out of.

I will not pray with any preacher in a robe.
Bad wind is what their wine won't wash away.
Who has his peace struck in a sudden light

lies stunned with luck and shattered love.
In a hundred fogs I've held my hands before
my face to catch ways the weather went,
always thinking there was time to change,
to be in wind the gull's tuning arc.

I've sailed my daddy's daddy's boat, worked
the same holes that fed them into men, who
both sank hard in simple beds and cursed
the life they left. No preacher makes
a man safe to see, in water, what he is.
I've prayed, for Christ's sake, breaking
wind in March storms that never raked
the leeches from my bitter heart, prayed
for nets not bagged with slime, but fish.
I know who found the man I thought I was
and he is sick for slants of sun playing
on a floor where children float like corks.
He prays to the stink of what's left to rot
when the tide is out on the black mud, to
wake himself for one more damned chance of
life. But that's not prayer. Maybe it is
not even hope, which never changed the wind
or put a lucky dollar in an old man's pocket,
or fished it out for a girl's gift in church
in the time before time howled headlong.

In Cumberland I had one uncle
who couldn't get out fast enough, so split
his head on the gearbox of a LaSalle.

He did not die but said he remembered the dark
was like it must be when you are keelhauled.

Beyond him, in your time, there was a man
with my own blood who leaped from a mountain
because the tiny river was too green to bear.

These are stories of outsiders choked up
with delusions and the downhill nights of mines.
I hope they have found a country to live in

as I stand sighing over the cat's fur of the sea,
thinking of you gone from Virginia, skidding
like a skimmed stone in the half-light of exile.

Because no one recalls how the murmur of water
called you from the hills, because the light
of farmhouse and sea towns blew out
at your coming, because you loved

the humped backs of dolphin and whale
more than mother or father, because in high gales
you knew what it was to go drunk in the ropes,

because the Labrador and the Gulf Stream whisper
their secrets to you like a friend, I stand
here naming each blade of grass

for one America drove into the sea,
that claw-sucking beast indifferent as haze,
licking the yellow onion of the moon!

Now they are become more than men we must know how
to tune up, to take
their flying root-and-stem light of joy
from each old hand as it pumps under the dunesigh
and liver-spotted leaf, learn
from lean gray men
hunched on a rail and singing to the waters the beauty
of breezeless gull-dotted dusk.

This one, his time come, nods, clamped jawbones
patient as a crab's,
years of notes loosed now, ear tufts and
silver hair drifting like streamweed, sways, pours
down his last gamboling sweat
for the world to out-
sing itself. Then another from the bed of his leg
lifts fiddle, begins to cuddle

and counterstroke the dying-out strain that a gone
grandfather sang to
the end like a man fearing God (so cries
the tune-whipped and untucked brother of their
right hand). When he buckles,
the next bows quickly
in feeling his boots already tapping the dark line
of the hewn fence. It must be

like entering a world where every breath turns dead
reckless and pure as gull
song tuned by nothing but ribbed sea light,
where hardheaded laid-down fathers rise up slowly
among crocus and bluebell as if
only minutes before
sleep whined like a gnat. And it could be standing
simply in the lightning-

like motions of such nameless, hardly to be believed
angels, we come at last
into the unfretting wish to be nothing else,
for there rises from bow's graze and struck strings
not only land's lute, but eerie rapture
stunning the sailor
who feels at first daybreak a peace slicing wrist-labor
as if before storm or prayer.

NIGHT FISHING FOR BLUES

Fortress Monroe, Virginia

The big-jawed Bluefish, ravenous, sleek muscle slamming
into banked histories of rock pile,
    hair-shaggy pier legs, drives
    each year to black Bay shallows, churns,

        fin-wheels, convoys, a black army, blue-

stained sequins rank after rank, fluting bloodshot
gill-flowers, sucking bitter land water, great Ocean
Blues with belly-bones ringing like gongs.

        Tonight, not far from where Jefferson Davis

hunched in a harrowing cell, gray eyes quick
as crabs' nubs, I come back over planks
deep drummed under boots, tufts of hair

floating at my ears, everything finally right
    to pitch through tide-turn and mud-slur
    for fish with teeth like snapped sabers.

        In blue crescents of base lights, I cast hooks

baited with Smithfield ham: they reel, zing,
plummet, coil in corrosive swirls, bump on
scum-skinned rocks. No skin divers prowl here,

        visibility an arm's length, my visions

hand to hand in the line's warp. A meat-
baited lure limps through limbs nippling the muck,
silhouettes, shoots forward, catches a cruising Blue

sentry's eye, snags and sets

case-hardened barbs. Suddenly, I am not alone:
three Negroes plump down in lawn chairs, shudder-
casting into the black pod plodding under us. One
ripples with age, a grandmotherly obelisk,

her breath puffing like a coal stove. She swivels
heavily, chewing her dark nut, spits thick juice
like a careful chum.
                    When I yank the first Blue
she mumbles, her eyes roll far out on the black-
blue billowing sea-screen. I hear her canting

to Africa, a cluck in her throat, a chain

song from the fisherman's house. I cannot
understand. Bluefish are pouring at me in squads.
I haul two, three at a time, torpedoes, moonshiners,
jamming my feet into the splintered floor, battling
whatever comes. I know I have waited
a whole life for this minute. Like purple dreams

graven on cold cell walls, Blues walk over

our heads, ground on back-wings, grind their teeth.
They splash rings of blue and silver around us, tiaras
of lost battalions. I can smell the salt of ocean
runners as she hollers, *I ain't doing so bad*
for an old queen. No time to answer. Two

car hoods down her descendants swing sinewy arms

in Superfly shirts, exotic butterflies: I hear them
pop beer cans, the whoosh released like stale breath
through a noose no one remembers. We hang

fast flat casts, artless, no teasing fishermen,

beyond the book-bred lures of the pristine streams,
speeded-up, centrifugal, movie machines rewound
too far, belts slipped, gears gone, momentum

hauling us back, slinging lines, winging wildly

as howitzers. Incredibly it happens: I feel
the hook hammer and shake and throw my entire weight
to dragging, as if I have caught the goddamndest

Blue in the Atlantic. She screams: *Oh, my God!*

Four of us fumbling in beamed headlight and blue
arclight cut the hook from her face. Gnats butterfly,
nag us: I put it in deep and it must be gouged out
like a cyst. When it is free, I hear Blues not yet

dead flopping softly. I tell her it is a lucky
thing she can see. She mops blood blued over
gold-lined teeth and opens her arms so her dress

billows like a caftan. She wants

nothing but to fish. I hand her her pole, then cast
as far as I can. She pumps, wings a sinker and hooks
into flashing slop and reels hard. In one instant both

our lines leap rigid as daguerreotypes; we have

caught each other but we go on for the blue blood of
ghosts that thrash in the brain's empty room.
We pull at shadows until we see there is nothing, then
sit on the shaky pier like prisoners. Coil after coil
we trace the path of Bluefish-knots backward,

unlooping, feeling for holes, giving, testing,

slapping the gnats from our skins. Harried, unbound,
we leap to be fishers. But now a gray glow
shreds with the cloud curtain, an old belly-fire

guts the night. Already the tide humps around

on itself. Lights flicker like campfires in duty windows
at Ft. Monroe. She hooks up, saying, *Sons they done
let us go.* I cast once more but nothing bites. Everywhere

a circle of Blues bleaches, stiffens

in flecks of blood. We kneel, stuff styrofoam
boxes with blankets of ice, break their backs
to keep them cold and sweet, the woman gravely
showing us what to do. By dawn the stink has passed

out of our noses. We drink beer like family.

All the way home thousands of Blues fall from my head,
falling with the gray Atlantic, and a pale veiny light
fills the road with sea-shadows that drift in figure

eights, knot and snarl and draw me forward.

Goshawk, Antelope

For Dee, & for Larry Lieberman,
always sustainers

Now, gently drowsing, she remembers the whistle blowing. It
surrounds space, time, sleepy summer evenings many years ago:
a remote sad wail involving sleep and memory and somehow
love. They'd fight on summer nights because it was hot and
Maudie cried and the icebox made a dripping noise, and because
the whistle blew. But they loved each other, and the whistle—
now it's a part of sleep and darkness, things that happened long
ago: a wild, lost wail, like the voice of love, passing through the
darkened room and softly wailing, passing out of the sphere of
sound itself and hearing.
—William Styron, *Lie Down in Darkness*

PART I   Messenger

For John Gardner

It was not kindness, but I was only buckle-high in the door.
I let him in because the knock had come, the rain
clawed each window and wall. I was afraid.
Climbing down the stairs I did not know
how my country, cunningly, had rotted,
but hear, now, my steps creak in memory
and the rocks let go in the blind night-glass
where you get up, frightened, to reenact
the irrational logic of flesh.

Even now I can't see why it happens, the moment of change,
but must try to witness each particular index
of landscape and irony of promise. I know
I was a child when the banging began, sleepless
with every light in the house blazing. Then
the man whose speech entangled me came in
from the mud world. He could not
put together the clear words of hope
we dream, only the surge of a river.
He, who said it wasn't a fit thing

for anyone, half-grown, to have to imagine in this godforsaken
life, said there was a message, the river high,
no chance. I remember the wind at that door
breaking like a father's hand on my face.
Such hurting does not cease and maybe
that is why the man went on fumbling
for love, for the loving words
that might be knowledge. He gave me

this message. I took it, and took, without warning, grief's
language that piece by piece has showed me how
to connect dreamed moments skidding like rocks
in the silence of a Wyoming midnight.
Each of his rainy words, fragments
of the old sickness, passed into me,
then he was gone, miserable and emptied,
and I had no home but the heart's hut,
the blistering walls of loneliness,
the world's blue skymiles of longing.

Common with drowned fir and uncoiling crocus, then, I
walked in ignorance and entered this terrible life
that was always a dream of the future
in the relentless unsleep of those
who cannot remember the last thing they wanted
to say: that love exists. And in darkness
you have dreamed me into your world
with their message, their words
whispering an hour before black, sudden knocking

that, even as I recall it, begins in your heart's meat
to reverberate, oh, its noise is going
to wake you like a dove's desire.
This is the dream of the soft buckling
of flesh, the beautiful last erosions,
and I swear I would give up these words
if I could, I would stop the code
of that streetlight just beyond your bed—

but it is too late, for the secret of hope swells in you
and who can stop the news that already screams
like the roof's edge leaving its nails

over your child's bed that is, now,
splintered and empty as every moment
skidding at the back of your neck? Leaves
not a month old hurl out of the storm
and steady splatter of time, and tomorrow
will lie still ripening, but only long enough
for you to catalog, in dream, what was possible

before the rake must drag its scritch-scratch over ground.
All I ask is that you turn to the child
inside, those words dreaming and changeless
as love's last chance—let them be said
against whatever, crying in the night,
we still think may be stopped, the black
historical fact of life's event
crashing, like a wall of water,
over the actuary's lawn and yours.

You have seen me before and would not hear, stung by your
wife's fierce beauty, when I called your name,
and the day your mother died I begged
your attention and got your dollar.
I followed you once, in New York, like truth,
always to give you the message, and now
on your porch, mud-spattered, I am
knocking to make you see what love is.
Call your wife, the police, anyone you like,

for everyone is waiting. We don't mean to be unkind but are
compelled to deliver, faithfully, the words
that have been fluttering in your ear
like a scream. It is not the wind
waking you, but the low roar of years

fumbling to tell you what has happened,
or will, when the door flies open
and the naked message of love
stands there stuttering in your face,
alive, crying, leaving nothing out.

The world has gone swimming in the night
and now, stepping from your bedroom,
you see the dream goes on without you.
As if you were only the quickened musk
of an ancestral trunk momentarily opened,
the dazzled world stands still to remember.
It is as if you were something and are now
almost something, but are not. Motion,
shadow half in memory. The world is full,
you are of this fullness, only you are
what the world cannot remember in first
raw light and nakedness. It waits a moment
like a woman shivering, dark water still
on her, ankle deep in mist, the sun purple
bright in each curve and coiling particular,
raking you with passion. Why have you lived
if not for this love? Only it waits in a cry
of elementals nothing explains, nothing,
and does not seem to understand you.
The world stares at you like a moronic angel.
That is why the rage crawls and the scream,
wordless as a night wind, pulls the lips back
on your sharp teeth. *Keep me, keep me, keep
me* the bird drills through pines playing
over the water. But this morning
your arm did not fall casually on whatever
you loved, your blood chilled. Now words
fail, or the world does not hear, and now
the slit of your dream fills with dust,
losing the shape you were, becoming
someone walking the path, waving good-bye.

Against snowpeaks, that country of blue sedge and shimmer
of distance rising into his tiny skull full of desire, he
fell across my windshield, a dot at sixty, and I, half-

looking for a place I had never seen, half-dreaming rooms
where blind miles of light lie on framed family faces,

saw him before he was anything, a spot above the glassy road
and in my eye, acetylene burned by brightness and hours
of passage. I saw memory. He came

out of the strange clouded horizon like the dark of whipped
phone wires and the quiet of first feathering shingles
in storm or in the hour of burial,

and dropped into absence where the antelope stood alive
at the fence of barbed wire, horns lifted slightly,
hovering on hooves' edge as if bored with the prospect
of leaps, long-standing and still. The wind-

darted dust gave no image beyond itself, puffballs that turned
clockwise and counterclockwise as he stood
changeless beneath that sudden whistle
of gray. I felt my heart

within those lovely shoulders flame and try to buck off
whatever the air had sent down as shapeless as obsession
and stopped my car, knowing already how
easily the talons dispossessed

all who, without illusions, lived. Dark and light bucked,
clung, shredded in me until I was again a boy on a fence,
hunched near the dream-contending world. But

someone far off was calling and I could not undream
what held me. Though I stood
at last it was late, too late. Someone
called and the legs I had always trusted broke
but not in time and I fell from all chance
to change what was done or undone.

In Wyoming, in June, it was already starcold
though the mild blue of dusk beat back my mother's pain
when I saw him, small as a wind, shriek for the cliffs,
his dream gone, the aching wingless shoulders of the antelope
risen from a low mound of rocks, running from what was
unseen and there, like the red print of a hand

about to fall, for I was late and wishing to God for a tree
to hide under and see for once what had died
out of my life but would never leave or
come back as it had been

like the slow growth of an antelope's legs into freedom
and away from desire's black whirling dream. It was
late, there had been no sign, no reason

to move except the call that might have been only dreamed,
but once I stood under the keening moon that, in Wyoming,
owns all that is and I begged the stars not to come
gouging my bitter and motherless sleep

where I lay long and longed, as I do now over barbed wire,
for the peace of the night-gleaming peaks and the flare
of absence that came, had fallen into

the accusing goshawk face of my father in that dark room
where I walked too late, where the glowing fur tufts
of candle shadows drift on her face and his

and what was held has become, suddenly, lost like breath.

Something has happened: the white meat of the shed siding
seeps, the snail's foot slickers from his house
lost in a week of red dust. Why is it

the earth gleams like the long-buried crown of a princess?
The stars, the stars stare down diffidently.
A pail by a well pours its emptiness.

Every night now the summons comes and something that
winks red as her first scarf and leaves, when she walks,
no longer hiss, for they are sapless and sodden

as the keening dead under the fieldstone floor of Virginia.
Something has been moving and she has heard it coldly
coiling like the creek, but it is not the creek

waking her from the dream. A gaudy blue flares in her face,
that explosion, and her match catches for an instant
a shape she cannot save, an eye that is

more memory than the gelatinous blue she long ago forgot
like the silky ghost of love. Is it, then, some lost gust
cracking her limbs? What marked her, entered

while the little patina of her breath was shining like ice
above the worn comforter? Is it only October's
dispassionate wind circling into her yard

and under the stars, come back as brutally clear as ever
to set the pail rattling with its gallon of darkness,
to send her out with God's name on her tongue?

Under the trees, until dawn, she will stand and not break
the stream of curses though the apples, star-bruised,
go on falling and do not kiss her good-bye.

From littered ground gnarled Winesaps have risen in drifts.
It comes, the faint sweet blood scent of rot comes.
It is October and nothing has happened.

What has happened to the stars? What thief, thin-soled
with rocks hard as seeds at flesh, has stolen them?
Surely something darker than the night,

the river shuffling aimlessly through the yawning toy box
of the universe, the cocked and stunned
right arm of the mechanical soldier,

has come red-eyed and drooling. It has happened before.

I don't mean to harp on the infinite paradoxes
there is no untangling, but why

have the stars come to rest on our feet,
on our soles bloody and crusted, those little
mouths that never speak what they meant to?

Perhaps it is only a cramp in our sleepless bellies,
the green apples we ate one hot afternoon.
The books have always warned us.

Lying awake in this moonless room
I think of stars like a crowd of pinched seeds
falling into the apples, sending little brass hooks
shooting through the white pulp.

By the time the apple's brown ache comes who will know
the stars have been stolen, who always rose
like fathers, in dignity, over the globes in the grass?

If I slide my heavy foot onto the floor, what
will fall from my chest? What will fall into my hands

heavy with the curving clarity of everything that is
not imagination and the filaments
of words charred beyond hope?

Something has happened in the black room while we were
flat on our backs trying to give birth
to the stars

and the books, in their shrouds, have slept through it.
Come to the window and I will show the world without
dreams, starless, mouthing itself, and the apples

growing black with nothing to tell us. Nothing.

In the place of the drowned, above the black sheen of a pond
giving its most indifferent shrug at dusk

you have seen this, but you did not see between shadows
what it was and the reason, simple enough,
wakes you in the sowing dark

where the leaves fester in storm. On the edge
of the willows leaning together like shy schoolgirls,
the silver flank of the sunfish

in molt the color of oatmeal still arches stiff and hurls
back the hot light streaming through the heart
of hill-warped trees, hurls and twists
from each scale set into position by
secret and implacable desire

a few flowing rays of light you saw but did not name.

They follow you into the bedroom calmly swimming
in that pulse of the far-off lightning.
The eye, glazed and womanly swollen, in mud

tilts now like a sinking rowboat as sheets of water climb
through willow and maple, and surely you sense
something as the nippling water sucks
down the hanging last drops on leaves.

The reason, oh, it is simple enough, but you can't understand
why this small ghost
should make you want to cry out to God

who, at the window, you have looked for as if you believed.
You have seen me, huddled by the woodshed, my apron
held fully over my face but the light behind
coming anyway clean through.

Here I am, me, sitting down in water and afraid to cry out
what I have seen and you have seen and nobody
understands, that enormous hunger.

I swear I will come back if you can tell me what it means
to hear the world belch its ugly answers clear as the truth
a child would be too scared to lie about.

The man with no name came,
his pants thick to the knees
with burrs, and he cradled
his face in his knuckles

and cried, if you can call
silence crying. One of us
spoke of dust on the sills
of the man's house. The lid

of light lowered, flattened,
birds darted. Across fields
the flicker of lamps began
but we stayed speaking softly

of the yellow faces of friends
in the dark, their suppers,
an empty chair. The man
backed into his steps, turned

from us, for we were not home,
kicked the dirt and then was
gone. Later we tried to name
the luck we had all had

in youth, dogs, field, love.
I remember him now walking
out of our bodies to touch
the dress with no music

in that box. I knew I would
follow him in my own time,
the dress was electric, his
knuckles white in that moon.

At the door when he comes
out of glowing stars, I say,
Lord, I don't know what to do
but go home, wash, and wait.

A pit as black as the secret bubble of a coal lump,
geode-brilliant and shimmering
as the heart's wet valves,

where a simple bird hungry enough to eat anything
would not go: this is something like what
I woke in, and there were many

of us hugging those walls, our mouths suddenly
open as if to say what we had always meant.
I wish I could tell you it was not dawn

with the sun's pale yellow racing down, for some
cannot believe death comes in the milkman's
hour or that it is, like the wife
in her gown, sleepless, out pruning the roses

although no one is expected. Have you
thought such a place could be,

without your knowing it, just there in your yard?
I don't want to alarm you, but the shadows flickering
through the locust so the green and gray

light falls on your face, what do they mean?
And is your child only sleeping

as precise as a glass statue this glary morning?

It arrives with no time to think of meaning, fever
like the blood streaks on the late bulbs

of wild roses there by the farm's rotting fence.
It is six-thirty and the cloudless horizon

of October hangs like a split-lipped laborer brooding
over his gun and the suddenness of his fate,

the same horizon running its moment through me, what
has happened changeless and painless as hysteria

in that empty and distant land we loved. I don't know
what is in the placid slick of your eyes

anymore, even when my hand lies down in the boiling
memory of your skin. We left you. We moved,

with dishes and debris sold, came here and no one
calls your name upstairs in the mild mean weather.

The creak and ball-bearing spin of bicycles fills
the street flaming with leaves. A cardinal jeers

for something hungrily alive in the limbs. I ask
you to think about the life we came away from

because I remember a moment I did not try to keep
which clings to me now, a time when your lips

flew apart in this violent light. Take your time.
I know you are far away and the sun is monstrous

through the slats crossed and ticked by wind
in the infinite instant that seized you.

Here they say such weather is unusual, cold and teasing
hours what we expect to get. I smile

expecting whatever comes, for the farm is far gone
and night keeps coming like the shot-to-hell look

in every face I see. Listen, I would run and never
drink another drop to hold that moment again, you

clenched and breathless in my arms as we went down
in the pond water that ballooned on your fever

before the moment came shaking me like a dog's jaws
loose from you, from the hour, from hoping.

Her. A quick and brittle music
as of harpsichord or bare feet treading
the cold deep of holly leaves.

The bones fell out of the bag
that was her skin.

They must make a sound like a suite
in a deaf composer's ear,
that tumbling

after the rush of sleep shattered.
Who stands by the river as we
stood, afraid of our bodies,
you already aching

for what we said before the dust?
The river lapped and seemed to love
all the things we could be.

Years ago, then, with a stick, I gouged
something green and she,

crying: *Let it go, it stinks.*
I teased her whom I loved, I swore
she was going to eat whatever
the river allowed us

and saw her eyes grow small and dart
in the shallows like small fish.
She gulped the river in.

It blew up her breasts that were white
with the first milk of her making.
The flood delivered her.

Below zero now, the sun dazzling snow
welds each watching eye to a slit.
Whose boy is this, whose somebody's
heart-rattling pain

goes with his stick to the waters?
I follow him and do not speak
for I would not want to have
to take that face in my hands,
wet with a green confusion.

We are all hungry, my mouth said.

Shyly, she seized my wrists, her mouth
opened to sing in a hard air,
then was gone, and all of us

with sticks trying to find her.

A gathering of dust, that gray piston from the world's
first balance insinuates everything and comes
down from blue-white croppings of rock
in Wyoming. Hoofprints fade, they
do not notice how they are

filled with that small body's cold summoning, but I see
that strange gesture which is like the swoop
of love, its corrective oscillations
without fear and beyond loneliness
that flies in my body and waits.

She spills over ledge walls like sunlight and is what,
in pinion and scrub oak, alerts the curled feet
for the running dream, the zero flight
that roots in the brain and lifts
each eye at the last, impossible

instant of fear. Through memory I follow its falling
and become what I was, a child playing in dirt,
my face up and frozen enough to see a hawkish
face in that second-story window,
that brightness of flesh

already wilting as it saw what it saw and understood
the earth's blunt deliberations. And I saw
through a handful of dirt I had thrown up
only shadows, shifting particles trying
to take a shape in the air. I could hear

not even one of the wordless cries out of her dream;
saw, but could not translate, that feather
flickering of her mouth, open, hungering
to lift me out of the world before
the dirt fell, slamming shut

the slits of my eyes. I saw her flinch as the shadow
came on her like a thing she had not thought
could be ours and now was. I did not know
why she cried out but began to howl
my child's tears

as if I knew what she knew, that the heart tears open
like the goshawk's mouth when it sees at last
what it has come for, but there is no cry
to outlast each cleft passage of rock
where a tongue of snow burns.

Long ago I saw that first wet glimmering of hawk tongue
and did not know, as I know now, the tiny scream
lingers only to say what has happened.
In pinion, already, eyes lift and are
too late, the heart chills and flakes.

Somebody had seen them from the highway,
had slowed for the curve which did not
betray its down-skidding slope
almost always, in that season,

thick with the black ice that gives nothing
the eye could whisper to the nerves.
Somebody used to them, carrying
a small wedge of salt

or maybe only some need to stop and look
into the night's moon-burnished bed.
After that he turned in sheets to say,
*Hundreds of them, some
down and dark as rocks.*

Not saying the black eyes flared, the hooves
chipped that snow to tiny explosions.

Not saying how the sheer air knifed lungs
as he lifted face to glare at the far peak
silent as God, unreal.

But later, when night clenched around him,
when memory flashed out of shadow,
he woke certain they had called

yet lay still and dark, afraid to look
where he knew there was someone
staring from the mirror.

And remembered then his sister and mother,
in homespun cloth the color
of blue wildflowers,
climbing that hill.
They turned, they waved, so tiny—

and kept eyes closed, for he knew lying
in ice-glazed ground they were gone.

What could he say if, summoned by the dark,
he should see a room full of antelope
and himself appallingly lost
in the slick holes of their eyes?

Hundreds, just standing. I don't know why.

Wrapped in a twisted brown stocking, strangled in the rolled
nylon of our grandmothers, it was wedged at the heart
of what little cool shade ever accumulated there.
You would have to walk out of your way, back
along an arroyo twisting and empty as memory, back
from the road out of town so far the sky itself
signals another world. To find it you do that,

though, in any case, you are simply walking and it appears,
something red shining through the gray-green glaze
of stunted limbs. If you were looking for a lost child,
your steps deliberate and slow, you might see it.
Otherwise you will go on. That is what we do.
But it waits to reveal itself, like an eye
in the darkness, and you may innocently look into that

moment, and may imagine why it lacks the slender heel which
must, once, have nailed many boys against a wall
where she walked. I kneel and pick it up
as you would, hearing though it is noon
the moony insects cry around her, hearing also
the nylon flake like pieces of skin against my skin,

feeling the sound of its passage from her shaven calf, a screech
like the hawk's when he is distant and not hungry.
In this arroyo no one could have seen her stop,
not as drunk as she pretended, sitting long
and, in time, methodically undressing, beyond
thinking now, placing her bundled shoe with care.
She must have been small and would have borne the usual

bruises, so we would have had no fear of any we might add,
when we stood smoking by the wall, catcalling lightly.
It would have been one of those nights the breath
aches it is so pleased with itself, then she
appeared in that red like the first cactus buds,
something clearly wrong with her but that, by God,
no concern of any red-blooded buck she might want.
In the junk car someone squealed, some rose
and fell. There were no names. I did not mean

whatever I said, but said it because she was so small, she
could not hide her fear and shivered on her back.
Such moments we tell ourselves to walk away from,
and we do, as now I have walked in my hoping
for absence, but there is no absence, only
what waits, like this shoe, to reach, to say please
as best it can for whoever comes along, as if forgiveness
were what it meant, and love, as if any weather
that red shining endured was the bruise
you might have kissed and might not yet refuse.

PART 2   Hospital Memory during Storm

For Robert & Michele DeMott

I

Time ticks everywhere and the stone, water-worn, takes
your testimony of pain like a smiling mongoloid.

Waking in the midsummer violence of lightning, you
find yourself naked and in need of the woman

who softly is there where you had, an instant before,
been certain witness of a terrible death.
Passion. And later, more than half in dreaming,

you cry out to damn the gnawing hours that tear
your memory of peace. The doctor

came, antiseptic, but he could not do what was required.
What is required? Have you after all these years
come to know that in any moment? Time, all day,
ticks like the sprinkler in your garden.

2

Under tubing that hangs and shines like gravity's spillage
your son opens his mouth to scream off the dog
suddenly looming at him five floors up, a raw
hole oozing under his eye. There is glass
and you turn to it, aware low-bellied cumulus

bruises black the running hills. In the hospital
faint bells toll a time which is not time
for the ordinary child skinned by a fall

as he hurries, late and sure of your anger, toward home.
Do you see him there, in the shadow's surge?
And what are you calling as you run?

3

His mouth sucks as if it truly loves the world and you
translate that shape of terror and say it
as love, as if love had not come too late.

Where are the right words? Who hears
what you have been trying to say? Ticks, time
does, in bubbling liquid, and you are murderous

when you see in his collapsed face the human image, meaty,
and seeping so when you think of this later it seems
the instant of no time, a dead-stopped
frieze that is everything.

At the edge of a hot night something is always waiting
unfulfilled, dangerously innocent, and probably
it has been a long time since you dawdled
into the luring dark. Probably

such an occasion returns when you pick up the pebbly Gideon
like your father's, finger-reading the words,
for though you are helpless maybe it will help you
hope the world is not deadly. Think this,
for maybe it will help you, though

the child, wordless, is screaming.

4

I must tell you there is no way for clinician or artist
to draw from that room the awful pus of death. If she,
dropping into her dream beside you, has conceived
or should yet, in the festery darkness,
do so, nothing will change. Headlines

in the morning paper are early set in sterile caps
above home snapshots. This is simple evidence.
If you have not thought out these things, it is time
to recall how you first encountered hope and what
risk you took for a plunge in desire
and a father's stare straight up at the moon.

5

The world gives no guarantee but of loss and life.
Love her now, wake her and do this, though she
may be as lost to you as the redolent
flowers in the vase. Hope's hunchback
sings from her sleeping and if you
pay attention you may recall your heart's faith
before memory and the wreckage of promise.

6

Do you think it is virtue to go on grieving, to wish back

forever that breath fluttered in a cage of small bones?
You too must hurry to get home and under the black
chance of falling night. Passion,
if you once believe in it, is a way of hope.

Between her teeth a weak current of air whistles. Though
her lips are dry, clearly she is lovely and has done
no wrong thing to bring down the lightning.
I urge you to turn to her while there
is time, before the dream returns,

for there is no child to stand stone-faced in your door.

GREENHEART FERN
For H.V.

Green
as rock-walled tide pools
we remember, shifting and transposing
itself like filigreed kelp sea-blossomed
in Keatsian dark even our best dreams must envy,
a simple plant with a spare grandmotherly thirst,
unlike yours and mine. But you poured anyway,
Lord how you poured. Then you moved it,
day after day, searching for light,
tracking every glow by a sextant,
some might have supposed,
under the soft gray
of your curls.

Like you, it went on
enlarging, sluffing off the dead
sores of self, of daily usage, fabular,
doing what it could to keep alive its house.
Each window got its share of your plant's attention.
Anyone driving by would have thought some green
invasion had caught us, would have said,
against radiant glare, we must be
slithering in a tangle of our
own making, though such
green was surely
luscious.

Today,
years from those tendrils,
from your finest lacy work at life,
I entered a house whose owner keeps plants
as you would not imagine anyone decently could,
rationing water as if it were castor oil and ignoring
the yellow sere of litter. In that room dark
as a clock's heart I heard the tick
of your breath's small judgment,
and almost, as I sat in a lump,
felt those fronds turn to me,
as if seeking the hands
cold and folded
I had for a week
forgotten.

It squatted in a grandmotherly yard,
surrounded by the breaking teeth
of a fence I left once
with a sheer tendril of skin.
It kept a dog whose folds of fur
held the rain and the dust
in a sweet comfort to me.
I remember falling suddenly
face to face with a creature
hidden behind its warped trunk,
her dark skirt billowing
with what must have been wind
but seemed the wild love
of an animal's shadow. She
lifted me to bed, cradling
my body like a crushed lily,
and I lay watching the tree
long after the dog disappeared
in the slow stream of the world,
long after her last steps
fled in a drift of small leaves.
This was no tree for the great
events, scarcely could sustain
the dream-weight of a boy,
and you could find scarred
in its flesh no deep initials,
but I remember its yellow berries
toppling silent and ripe,
how the day I walked out
they burst into bright tears.

These were the crushed fruit
of no worth, then as now,
clinging to the shoes
that pinched grown feet,
staining every least fabric
with that awful stink
not quite human, not of earth.

On my back, shirtless and with no friend, in September
when the time is for a young man to have seen breasts
only slightly larger than his own, thinking of her
who is inexplicably older but was not

not an hour before: to have seen that then like a purple
bruise (that strange) through the gaunt, stretched-neck
loop of her T-shirt stained by wrestling, I tell
you I felt the tick of grass and itch-weight

of earth and thunderous roll of the Missouri gathering
downhill toward the ocean; and thought then, as I ate
from all silence the green bitter grapes that were
by my grandmother forbidden, being poisoned

to ward off disease from Arkansas, for the first time
that I would rather be dead than not to be alone
with what I had seen, savoring her as sunlight
curved through the grape leaf. If ever in

that bed of rocks I feared what held those hard nubs
inviolate might eat my guts out or wished some other
season, cold or wet, had kept me from the accident
of what was, I cannot recall. There was sun,

a little wind, a space of ground yellow with dandelion,
that throb of passage, fracturing shadows, grapes
with no name. Once, then, I floated in a world
I knew to be infinite, delicious, itself

churning and speaking through the voice of each shadow
and juncture of light. After that I slept, improbably
dreaming I stood in a center of light, and woke
in the dark, godless and afraid, alive.

Tonight in the hills there was a light
that leaped out of the head
and yellow longing of a young boy.
It was spring and he had walked
through the toy-littered yards
to the edge of town, and beyond.
In the tall spare shadow of a pine
he saw her standing, she of skin
whiter than the one cloud
each day loaned to the long sky,
whiter even than the pure moon.
But she would not speak to one
who kept her name to himself
when boys laughed in the courtyard.
He watched her burn like a candle
in the cathedral of needles.
After awhile he saw the other light,
the sun's leveling blister, bring
its change to her wheaten hair.
In growing dark he waited, certain
she would hear the pine's whisper,
counting on nature's mediation.
But she would not speak and even
as he watched she vanished.
Slowly he knew his arms furred
with a fragrant green darkness
and as the moon cut its swaths
on the ground, as trucks rooted
along the road of colored pleasures,
he felt his feet pushing through

his shoes, his hair go sharply stiff.
He could hear her laugh, could see
her long finger loop a man's ear
but this did not matter. Already
he felt himself sway a little
in the desert wind, in the wordless
emptied gnarling he had become.

What do you want to go back to?

If you think of it the vision comes, the day
bright as an arc welder's sizzle,

and you know the plump sound of single drops
of rain, staccato in a gutter,
don't belong. They mean another place.

The frail drift of a flute idly played
is only an illusion displaced from the other
days when, with the window open,

the river grayly hugged its hood of ice.

Therefore, you look harder for the leaves
growing silver-sided with butterflies
and some kind of animal waiting
with eyes wet and crystalline

as geodes under a flowing foot of water,

and the long white forearm of a valley declines
to a palm where the cloud's shadow floats
in the color of a lost nickel.

There is a face printed in the flesh of your thumb.

If, face down in the soft huzzahing of grasses,
you feel the earth breathe and the pulse

run time through each tendril's
coil, the itch

of unwashed children comes in a blush
before the assault of suffering.
In this moment, call out your name.

If you do this, you will have some idea of what
passes in the nervous system of dandelions
and in the eyes of love

once shocked wide in the welding sun.

Ribbed with red glitter, those glass studs catch
and hold the early lights my mother
has raised in her longing. Her
hands waist-high cradle my one
gift, lovingly, while behind
her shapeless black suit
the shragged green
of the little cedar hides
in the brilliant blinking of bulbs.
Out of the light, in the dark crooked
arm of the stairs, I wait and want
to enter the room where she is. I am

still a child, though already I know the meaning
of snow on the high hall window, that
incessant pecking like sand
the wind whips out of darkness,
piling it up until there is
no place and no time
except for the moment
glimpsed, as through glass,
deep inside the snow wash.
This year the tiny Jesus hangs
in a matchbox and the tree
wears raveled strips of news-
paper bearing names of the dead.
My naked feet slide on cold wood,
I feel my way down the dark,
for I do not want to hurry

to find her in the middle of that instant ice-
bright and all there will be of Christmas.
Long ago she called but I dawdled
in my bed to see how thin was
the white bulk of breath,
wanting and not wanting
to know how poor we had become
with a war raging and a father gone.
By each step I have grown larger
in her waiting, but am still
only a boy with no gift
except words

that, in memory, bristle and are evergreen as light
from a sparse bush she hacked and stood up
that night. I give them back now,
remembering how long it takes
to come into this loving

room where she stands for me,
her face, in sepia, slightly bent
over the white holster. The gun
suddenly silvers like a long stroke
of whirled snow before her body
and I see, now, she holds
my gift, the leather
stiff and white, the red tears
of glass, the black fake fur
in tufts making a pony's shape.
Her arms, light-bruised, extend

as if from the cedar's delicate, bent spine,
its fur and her dress one dark

blinking, as now my eyes open
and shut on that image. Words
fill that room with the rush
of needles gone crisp in time.
They sweep me into her arms,
words that lace the dark memory
of joy to the particular glint
of her hand on my hair. *It is
what you wanted isn't it. He said
in his last letter you would want it.*

Overhead tonight, in snowless December,
the stars blink quiet explosions.
Their bursts fall endlessly
on shoulders of rock and skirts
of cedar, until there is no square
inch of earth that does not gleam.
At stair top, with hand flat
on the wall, switch off now
so the tree squats alone,
I remember the long light
pooled on the floor,
that flesh and black suit
I must come down to.
All day I will draw guns,
deep in a child's joy,
shaking the cedar like a bomb.
Happy, I will shoot at her, *happy,*

until at last the words bang
from her mouth as she holds me,
saying, *Yes, yes, yes.*

Among milkweed, in the wide-shaking wind
that unlocks each eye, the carpenter
stops, his board balanced
on his shoulders. Something triggers

the river light on the underedge of leaves,
the flat ringing of helpers' hammers
looms in delicate song. The term
of his mourning circles back

on itself. *Hey,* he shouts to the roofers.
Her hair is in his eyes, its falling
at her waist in starlight, music
he suddenly begins to dance to

as if it were not that black force pooling
under the C&O slag heap, not the dream
murderous among the crickets where
she, so long, had lain

humming in his ear. The glint in the green
is like wedding silver flushed
from mud and roots, and it clicks
for that first usage—his ear

lives again and immediately the board whirls.
Out of the darkened eye of the earth
he becomes the dreamed self rising
back to life and the moment

spreads into the shadowy faces of helpers.
On roofs, under timbers, out of trucks
they see the miracle of absurd light
spinning from his body

and there is not anything to keep off now
their need to leap up from the nails,
to cry back, *Hey,* though each one
tomorrow will not remember.

And he, when he falls dizzied and sinking,
will think it was only a dream that,
in the long madness of labor,
would be heartbreaking if it lasted.

Through the small door of a hut
he stares at us, our movements,
the thousands of faces we are,
the booming world's roar

that, later, for a drifting instant,
he will enter. His extra shirt
tied by its arms for a sack,
he will be lost in his luck.

By the freeway, whipped as a weed,
he stalks the malignant ground
for bottles, and we wear on.
He doesn't imagine anyone

weeping in anger as he looms up.
And when he comes to the truck
parked, the woman asleep inside,
he thinks of his nights, wide

as the blue glare on the concrete,
full of glass and the clink-clink
of his business. For him sunset
is the good hour, the shapeless

beams of headlights always thick,
blending with sun to flick
off what he hunts. He is alone,
himself, dreaming of the blown

treasures of the world, the bottles
like loaves of gold. The rubble
of everything falls about him
like snow. He bends, reaches, grins,

and ignores whatever we scream.
His tarpaper walls are the dream
he has given himself. At night
a wind plays over the pipes

he has fashioned from glassy mouths.
The world seems right, as he lies out
in bed, but fingers itch, and a face,
oh, whose is it, leans, leans like grace

and he can't remember whose or why.
At dawn, aching, he watches the sky,
sees dark birds pass, then us,
and is himself again, staring, blessed.

Mercifully, the sun spangles on the tile and on
my closed eyes, spilling that unlooked-for
and dusky forgiveness that fog, for days,
denied us. I roll myself in the sheets,

trying to come up out of the blindness of a dream's
drift and whirl. I can hear gulls and children
far off, blooming, the world I walked away
from years ago, but I am not the one

walking out of the surf. Somehow I have slipped,
like the seal, down into the root tangles
of dream. Phosphorous rocks loom and glitter
above me, breaking the sun in pieces

each with the shape of those I've loved and mourned.
With them I want to give up exile and rise
in their gold looming, seeing at last
how they hope for this to happen,

so cry out and become a child who discovers himself
alone in the house for the first time.
I fling my small sounds against the walls
where parents were, just now, and try

to beg back everything that, slowly, has been moving
off into the shadows of the rocks. Like you
I have found myself where I never was, dream-
drowning and entering the memory

of all cries made by the sudden cramp of love,
feeling my heart swell against each rib
of a remembered light. In this room
and in the fusing eyeblink of morning

I roll and make the cries until her face finds me, finds
my lips cool in the delicate hair on her neck.
This is what I have waited for, the body
of joy buoyant with forgiveness, all

bodies seal-sleek rising from the fracturing waters.

The green mothering of moss knits shadow and light,
silence and call of each least bird where
we walk and find there are only a few words
we want to say: water, root, light, and love,
like the names of time. Stunned from ourselves,
we are at tour's tail end, our guide long gone,
dawdling deep in what cannot be by any human
invented, a few square miles of the concentric
universe intricate as the whorls of fingertips.
The frailest twigs puff and flag in the giantism
of this elaborate grotto, and we are the dream,
before we know better, of an old grotesque
stonecutter who squats under a brow of sweat,
the afternoon a long glowing stalk of marble.
We have entered the huge inward drift behind
his eyes and wait to become ourselves. We stare
through limpid eyes into the vapor-lit past
where breath, wordlessly, like a near river
seams up, seams in and out and around darkness.
Somewhere far back in the hunch of shadows,
we stood by this wall of vines, and he, angry,
froze us in our tracks and the blade of belief.
That tree there bore the same long slithering
of light from a sky he owned. Disfigured now,
its trunk rises thick and black as a monument
that rings when struck. Here the hiking path,
a crease, stops, then spirals around into stumps.
Our party has gone that way, stumbling quietly.
From time to time, someone calls out but we know
only the words whispered from the wall of leaves:

water, root, light, and love. We stand silent
in the earliest air remembered, hearing at last
the distant and precise taps of the mallet
until our clothes, as if rotted, fall away
and the feckless light fixes us on the column
of our spines. Without warning, we begin to dance,
a bird cries, and another. Our feet seem to spark
on the hard dirt as we go round the black tree
and for no reason we know we see ourselves
throwing our heads back to laugh, our gums
and teeth shiny as cut wood, our eyes marbled,
straining to see where it comes from, that
hoarse rasp of joy, that clapping of hands
before which we may not speak or sing or ever stop.

PART 3   Settlement

For Norman & Jody Dubie

For after all, a gale of wind, the thing of mighty sound, is
inarticulate. It is a man who, in chance phrase, interprets the
elemental passion of his enemy. Thus there is another gale in
my memory, a thing of endless, deep, humming roar, moon-
light, and a spoken sentence.
—Joseph Conrad

The vision of dreams is this against that,
the likeness of a face confronting a face.
—*Sirach 34:1–3*

Wind lifted the curtains and I saw how far
it had come to enter my dream
of the story she was telling.
Out of the brown distant
mountains, from grassy shadows,
farther than I had ever been,
it came and lay nudging
the scrolled, hand-stitched
linen hung by her mother
over logs, then these windows.

She did not tell me about desert wind or
why she had to take me back
through her gathering of dreams,
the stained faces, hands no more
to me than iced footsteps
left in the winter.
Now, in my own overheated room,
the grease-flecked plates
wait to be stacked and I
sit by myself and begin to know
they memorized me and took me
into the lost black
geographies of their bodies.

They were poor, they ate whatever might be
found, wormy bread, sometimes the dead
worms burrowed in a green crust.
That room was big, though spare,
dark molding whose varnished

promise had long ago spidered
still gleamed like a cave's
footpath where I was
summoned, small and cold
in my swallowing
against the clear early light.

In one corner of the airy room she is rocking,
fawn hair gone gray in slight drifts.
Her legs cross at ankles, housed
in the anonymous black skirt.
Her blouse hangs ice-white
as snow curved, sometimes,
against the leaded glass.
The rug, red but with deep blue
curlicues of wool, betrays
the worn tread of boots
to the squat stove.

Today it is August, so hot
breath waits in the mouth.
She has been reading for hours
but, now, at some passage, stops,
her forehead damply beaded, to tell me,
Books are all lies and no help.
A chestnut colt throws its voice
against the barked corral that will,
before the first snow, collapse.
The great book falls from her lap
with the popped sound of flesh
struck, and I know it means
she has fallen into the rooms
of the old people lost

in house dust and yellower than paper.
We have sure God seen bad times.

The book, in my memory, is like her
judgment but was no more than
a small roof splayed over no walls
like the useless napkin on my plate.
It was a world of glorious stories
with horses like the two
thick-coats her father left us
and men who did not choose
the swords that cleaved joy
like my own Wyoming stars.
Loyalty was a thing I understood
as she twisted me through words
plain as that open room.

She did not tell me how they passed into
the settlement of dust always
weaving through the windows
to dull the flash of uncut hair,
how the portrait of our ancestor,
in tunic and empty scabbard,
unjeweled, would go on
flaking around the painted
blue shock in the eyeholes.
But with crash of steel
that face would swing
down a hillside she made
enormous and green until
I stared into the horizon
where I might someday cling
to a nag's mane in small glory.

Let us pray. And I would squint, not wanting to leave
all the light, as her prayer mumbled
backward crazily to freeze a man
who led a mule and a broken mare
through the night paths, moonless,
over the Shenandoah fieldstone, not
stopping for fear of deserter's rope,
into blistering miles of light
already our memory. No more
than a shrug of his meaningless
thrust into history, she
prays him, or someone like him,
to forgive her despair, tears
on her cheek and on mine
the same bright, last glimmer
rising from these leftovers at dusk.

Outside the wind grinds leaves in the street,
leaves face to face tumbling,
clinging for an instant
and I am afraid I cannot well
remember her rough palms deeply
stained by the ground I loved,
but remember the crow-darting
of her eyes, the vision
of a man with a woman, both
in fear on the moonscape of prairie,
mouths wide to sing as they
scoured with sand the cache
of pewter plates. Fire flare,
for awhile, defined them

as I, in my mind, am defined by a moment. I
stood, not only in my own body, but
armored by dream and glow of noon
in an arroyo fleshed with first
gaudy flowers of cactus, and knew
in the midst of cavalry charge,
imagined, the green odor of
water. It was, suddenly, there—
the speech of the world—
it cried out, *Believe!* I did,
and did not think how she,
at window, would have seen
the sun withering all
I loved beyond image or word.
In that moment, I think, I felt
the tuned, single sway of prayer

trying to pass through the curtain of my skin.
I ran through the gouged trench,
certain snakes skittered before
the sunburst of my toy pistol,
until I rested at the flume
end of rocks, ashen, and
then climbed on a nag, cataracted
and stolid, to kick his laboring
ribs until they bled. My heart,
in joy, beat without effort,
as I roared in significant battle
against myself and the scar
of our house, white in that place.
The goshawk rolled overhead
as if he knew the carrion
I would leave. Later I sat

on the wooden circle of rails
to see him bend the air,

ruthless in his unwill, as tonight I sit in words
plummeting down through my head
to enter again the room
where my mother is trying
to lay out the act of settlement.
But cannot get there, quite, for
I have only left the corral's height
to lean on my grandfather's last
post whose nail, raw and thick,
waits still to be struck, and sings,
sometimes, in the night wind.
From here I see the window,
the wing of the chair,
but no face over the red and blue
rug like a desert orchid, no
hands translucent

that must come down on me like a hawk's shuddering
all the way through my wing blades
for what I have done, no man
yet, though man-tall and cruel.
Here I remember the knight,
the story beginning everywhere,
words wandering in frail paths
full of campfires and droppings
of ghostly horses. A queen's crowned
bones glow from her face, and soon
a castle, clammy, will rise,
a crumpling oak fire inside,
and downhill a shady village.

The stone floor is mantled
by knight's boon, a rug
whose creatures livingly weave

what I most understand, the shelter and sacrament
that make her voice keen and tingle
like an antelope's as she dives
under the dark's shoulder. Gray,
in quick glints like a goshawk,
the man comes, leans, kisses
her forehead. Then
I am born. Then the man,
like a thought, breaks or leaves,
and we are alone in the dust
of words, fingers racing the lines
as if, sun-blind, we have come
at last to the last rock
and the level horizon red, now,
as her handprint on my flesh
that has settled deeply in—

Why do you do it? I sit toying with a knife
in the food I do not want, trying
to answer, but lost as always
in the bright bloom of cactus,
in the surprise I take
from the flanks of a blind horse
whose knifing squeal rides
up my arm like joy's word,
only it is not, and the blood,
like grease, scabs my touch
until I do not know what
I believe or believed—

but know her voice licking out
in hawk shadow to snag,
like a nail, whoever might
pass in the arrogance of dream.
Well, what have you learned
in your God-blessed wandering?

At the end must life seem so unreasonable,
the hawk's screech faint as snow rasp,
coal's soft inward settling
that leaves the armored stove
empty, the room dusted blue?
I went in the world and she
remained in that place
where I had grown to no answer,
our lessons unfinished.
But received, in time, the summons,
mailed by a man who wandered,
they said, but good with a hammer.
I went too late. The house
stunk like a hut so I lunged
angrily at the swollen window,
the rooted frame refusing, and
burst elbows through glass.
The few drops on the rug,
long ragged, went brown.

I sat in her rickety chair and, for a time,
slept, and no dreams. Then woke
cold, cramped. She had
no wood now and no coal.
I took up the tattering blue book,
making a fire of its pages,

clawing them out, only the sewn
and deepest still whole,
the rest shriveled and sere.
I had not thought to bring food
so drank the gin quickly,
not a word spoken. Then wind,
with the light scent of—was it
cactus?—came, and I dreamed
a far cleft of rock, a man
trying to pull something
from the darkness of stone.
I woke in the memory
of weaving fingers,
the cathedral, that whistling

when the world stared in its empty abstraction
and terror, what she taught me.
I had been afraid one night,
sleepless in the grave desert
that stalked each window.
She had climbed the black stairs,
calling ahead to comfort me,
and in dead dark, bookless,
made each sound of each animal
the knight kept alive in his
rug and the house of his heart.
I blew hard for that music
but tucked my cold hands
under armpits and listened
all night to the rattle of glass
like teeth, to an agitation
of wind at our door

that was, perhaps, only the boiling of dust
and lopsided hilling of the world's
words—all she had left me,
as now the leaves outside scrape
in a language I almost understand,
the night-splintered whisper
of longing. Is that it? Almost
I hear a man and a woman
speak to me from far back,
offering words like fire-sizzled
chunks of meat to one hovering
in darkness, a glint only.
I do not know what they mean
but take what is given now
without judgment or promise,
letting it whistle up
whatever shape or shade of love
the wind will settle on me.

And now I think of that curtain lying
like a skin between my body
and all the world.
I think of the man with a hammer
tapping down the dark
blinding boards, as leaves,
this night and every night,
nail against my window
their decomposing palms.
For this and the words for this
she prayed, and I will pray
that all remain what it has been
in communion of dream, except
for the scummed eye

that horse turned on me
as if he who could not forgive,
forgave — knowing I would
ride him forever,
knowing the endless, indivisible
miracle we were in that place
would be unspeakable as a wind
in the throat's deep
where it is.

So then in the morning we would wake,
the steam of summer on us,
sheets kicked back,
and out of whatever dream
we had been floating through
our mouths would open and lazily
cup the air as if it were forever
the water of love's sailing,
and it would begin again.

Your hair in my hand drifting,
the dark odor of pine pitch, that
silent sizzle of light on our skin
would return, would be the bell
and curve of your breast, sudden,
then the slow saw droning
each of its brassy teeth
over the distances of water.
We would see the child—
almost—that face we tried
to conceive out of the instant
before time sent the sound
of labor's breaking,

and I would ask what face you had seen,
in this birth of the imagination,
until you would cry no, no,
until the dream we rode
like a farmer's horse
became two and we would fall,

whoever we were, staring
through the tiny attic window
at the blue emptiness where
birds jeered their confusion.

So we would lie in the split vision
of that moment which is everything
memory gives us, trying to know
the nature of love, hearing
it begin with the horses
in the near fields of June,
hearing their naked whistle
like startled upriding
birds, not knowing
where, in what swoop of joy,
we might rise or land or what
hardness, again, was beginning.

In the yard the plum tree, wild
with a late summer wind,
shakes its thousand planets
of sweet flesh.
Does it mean to resist
this gush that drops
one order of things
into another? It keels,
leaning at forces we can't
see, can't know the edge of.
Its memory keeps only two
commands: this lives, this
dies from the licking sun.
There is no metaphor
to reveal what it has known
in its brooding years.
We watch the purple fruit fall
as leaves shear and snap
and nail themselves to light.
Between us the wind
is a word seeking a shape,
hovering in passion
and risen from the ground
of memory clenched
in roots and long tendrils.
Hearing that, knowing ourselves
wingless and bestial, we wait
for the sun to blow out,
for the return of that first
morning of pink blossoms

when we saw the dark stains
of our feet printing
what we were on that
dew-bed of the world.
The tree, too, waits
in its old unraveling
toward a naked silence,
its language wild and shocked.

Today, bitch of a day, trembling
false light on everything,
the promised change
is not: dusk rounds corners,
a newspaper under its arm, gray
overcoat flapping, one thing
to count on beside self's sickness,

snow remembered foul with ice,
hunched in the aborted grass
like terror, one snaking
tongue flares in a small bush
lost in winter. You try, can't
hold it. The window's iced.

Hold still now: the diva
no one ever expects comes
into your room, hanging
plants rustle, coilings, tendrils
almost music; the aquarium bubbles
with biting shadows, rhythmic
wakes, and still her voice

breaks with static, she goes.
On the table the hulls of salt
and pepper shakers, tracks
in what you poured out
circling on themselves, playfully
at first, then desperate for what
was the beginning: suddenly

the fierce blaze of light, her
cry riding the one long note
of your breath, the overcoat
left in a corner, and you
know a surge in the earth,
something trackless, nor of wires
received, envelops you, is

and is gone with the shift she
rides, the beautiful diva
straining notes like moments
so rare nothing dies. Who
would not risk everything
for this, even as darkness rushes
over the fish, the salt, the snow?

I imagine her trying, trying to catch it. First,
dusting dutifully, slow now for the child
leans heavily under her dress, she finds
the web behind her hand loom. Her frail
hands mean to weave a birth cloth, but time
has speeded up on her. On her face, the worst

black shadow crawls and squats and waits. At last,
delicately, she moves the loom to discovery.
The black spot hunches in the black heart
of the corner, snoozing in maternal reverie.
Her hands, now, shake. The web gleams like art.
She feels heavier, her fast blood slows to paste.

An hour later, pulse loud as a truck, she kneels
with the glass jar and strikes out at it.
Legs black as a satin dinner dress uncoil
and dance her back in memory to moves quick
still in her body. Clumsy, afraid, she fails
the first time, then screws tight the metal seal,

but punches a small hole for air. All afternoon
she keeps it in the refrigerator, admiring
that red jewel she cannot bear to smash.
Home from work, a husband, I find the thing
is mine to kill, like memory. She won't watch.
In the yard the sun boils, the sky is sheer blue.

I tell her it is a small thing she must put away
like clothing in a cardboard box. I hold her,
driven to distance by the swollen bulb
of her womb, but she cries and shivers.
At night she wakes from dreams of a world
shatteringly bright and of her girlish waist

gone, with my foot on it like an executioner. She
swears she's full of spiders, still half
asleep, and kicks the blankets off to lie
naked in a little light like an hourglass.
Accused, I sink in my own dark, the itch-glide
on my skin the fear of what she bears and flees.

Under the pitched roof
of a single leaf
I have come to
the forgiving place
my body may hide in.
The rain speaks
its soft German
through a frayed
bronze moustache
whose wings,
when I arrive
and am still,
quiver into an end-
less angling of stories.
My father, that sobbing
inventor of all,
has come out
from under the gray
wheezing house pipes,
the mud of his plumbing
quick with rain.
Guttural as a tyrant,
he pulls down
each leaf's lovely
palm and cups me
into a floorless room.
Through each stem neck
and tongue of vein,
he sings at the world's
outrageous heart,

that accuser,
to whom we are
the inexplicable things,
the loved debris.

In the backyard, by the stilled
oscillations of the cheap
metal fence defined
by the weight of children,
the small maple
waves in the first
gusts of a fall day.
Behind breath-frosted
glass, hearing far off
my child's cry, I
see this waving become
my father's thick arms.
He waves at the ballgame
where players swarm
at his call. One spits.
He waves from the nose
of a rowboat, drunk
with fish and ashamed.
He waves at the black
end of a treeless street
where my mother has turned
from the house, crying.
He waves on a little hill
above the playground,
his whistle shearing
over each knuckle
of asphalt. When I stop
running, out of breath,
he is still there, waving,
and I am waving, beating

the air with my arms,
sored and afraid,
and there is no wind, only
the brilliant distance
like a fence between us,
waving and waving.

In this season, through the clear tears
of discovery, my son calls me
to an abandoned barn. Among
spiders' goldspinning and the small
eulogies of crickets, he has entered
the showering secret of our lives,
and the light fur of something
half-eaten mats his hands.
Later, on a rotting length
of pine, we sit
under the star-brilliance
of swallows fretting
the hollow light.
Under them, dreamless,
we have come to cast
our lot with their songs
of celebration.
All afternoon we sit and become
lovers, his hand in mine
like a bird's delicate wing.
Everywhere the sparrows go down
to the river for the sweet
tears of communion. Soon,
in the yellow last light,
we will begin again to speak
of that light in the house
that is not ours, that is only
what we come to out of the fields
in the slow-plunging knowledge
of words trying to find a way home.

PLAYING BALL

Last year there was no chance.
You stared into the empty
blue as if into a room
you were afraid to enter.
So we begin, in a tangle
of absences, to know
the shapes that wait for us.
Now alone in the grass
gone green only for us,
I wave you away, seeking
the right distance until
somehow you understand and go
and are there, yourself—
that I remember and turn
away from for the first time.
These strokes are easy,
just enough to make rise
the thing you will lose
in sunlight and in fear.
I watch how you tumble
toward me, the tattering
glove of your fathers
too large, your face opening
at that deceit and the earth's
unpredictable, quick skid.
A mockingbird sits on a bench
to scout whatever moves.
He catches more than you do
but has nothing to say,
having no chance to become

the beautiful secret thing
you are, calling for more
in the high hard sun.

That flock of starlings hewing the air
above the orchard is nothing
but the strangling of desire.
I know their country is nowhere
and would not throw a single stone
against such beautiful longing.
They have walked out to be
at the heart of our bodies
and cannot find what they want,
or even a gleam from the gone sun.
Under them I bend down quietly
and pick up a black feather
as if it were the dropped scarf
of my sleeping daughter. Holding
this for hours, I find myself
unable to say a simple word
true or false, until I become
the little thing my body is
in the hiding fur of a woods.
Then I look across the hedgerows
at the foreign light of my house.
Somewhere in the distance of dark
a voice is calling my name,
but not too loud, and I want
to fly up and gather the last
radiance of the sun and take it
like a song down to her mouth.
Oh, daughter, in the thick trees
where fruit bruises beyond joy,
I hunch among the starlings,

folding and unfolding my love,
afraid for the black wing of silence,
for what must wake in each voice
when it swirls up at daybreak
so naked, so uncertain, so lost.

Flying from the end of my
boot, my daughter's cat,
and the tame quail gone
up in a spatter of feathers,
to leave me turning there
as the dew dulls out, bare
shoulders flushed from that
quick sprint, the back door
still banging like a ripped
shred of memory. I think
I can hear the world grind.
Like a man in a car
that's just dropped something
to howl down a quiet street,
I am saying, *Please, please,*
and only mean I want to
go on wherever I am going,
and want the trees to remain
a close, shadowing green
tunnel without that light
banging hard overhead and
do not want, for God's sake,
to hear this slow gouging
of sparks that is the world,
the intense unloosening stare
in the cat's eyes as I loom
out of the sudden stillness,
the fixed and heart-dark
pupils of the child startled
to see what cruelty is, always

to know this first dream of
love's division. I am crying,
Please, oh, please — not
wanting this to happen, this
sun the color of a cat to fall
on her struck face that is
learning to mouth these words
without end, with only
a beginning already long lost
like pawprint or feather
where grass goes stunningly
dead, and sun, like flint, strikes.

Night-black in the yard begins to glow, then shakes
the oaks heavy in sleep like an old dog's thighs.
This wakes a bird whose belligerent advance up limbs
reshapes the world we have known. His notes announce
what was left the day before, tricycle, toy, tree,
the newsworthy unchanged. Assiduously he sings
to make things so. He names. Hearing him, I break
from my bed of dark anxiety and the dream of a girl
sobbing at dusk for a favorite stone she's lost.
Like him, cries were all she had to summon back
her piece of the world. The scene replays and I see
I followed her up stairs, promising it all intact,
and lay me down on the toy-littered stage for prayer.

It's there I return at first light, and heavily wait.
The bird, encouraged by his story, tells another
louder than the first, making her bear blue-eyed,
bringing the breath of day to jingle her hung puppet.
He makes the dark retreat in every room, a sad light
ring the halls, as if he were meaning's journalist.
I, on the floor, lie listening, stone-numb, and ache
at every inflexible angle of being, unable to rise,
hopelessly beyond any whistling I made in the dark,
more and less than song, for her. He pursues his work,
outlining house and car, alley and insomniac. This
chatter is what it takes. I watch her face float up,
bright, round as truth itself. Light's here, known.
The news goes on, her cat's at the door and mews,
dusk's color, a garbler at best, his intention unclear.

She leaps me by a yard, is gone, a far door slamming,
out into the somewhere of the grass, defining the fur
of a cat while I count what I'd gathered in her sleep:
a small kingdom of stones. All morning I think of her,
of rooms she cracks through like light and the gleaming
ground she sifts not for the lost but the not-found.
And think, too, of the bird hunkered in green shadow
and silent, concocting words for a world full of cats.
Note by note by note we arrange what's known for song
while trees tower over us, spreading a storied gray-
gold that keeps what must be found, lost, and found.
At dusk I throw the stones back in the yard. The bird
makes his inventory, the oaks yawn and settle like saints.
All night stones glow like eyes, or like nothing
we could dream, unnamed, each a promise we must keep.

PART 4

The Roundhouse Voices

In memory of Ralph G. Smith & Lloyd Cornwell

In full glare of sunlight I came here, man-tall but thin
as a pinstripe, and stood outside the rusted fence
with its crown of iron thorns while
the soot cut into our lungs with tiny diamonds.
I walked through houses with my grain-lovely slugger
from Louisville that my uncle bought and stood
in the sun that made its glove soft on my hand
until I saw my chance to crawl under and get past
anyone who would demand a badge and a name.

The guard hollered that I could get the hell from there quick
when I popped in his face like a thief. All I ever wanted
to steal was life and you can't get that easy
in the grind of a railyard. *You can't catch me,*
lardass, I can go left or right good as the Mick,
I hummed to him, holding my slugger by the neck
for a bunt laid smooth where the coal cars
jerked and let me pass between tracks
until, in a slide on ash, I fell safe and heard
the wheeze of his words: *Who the hell are you, kid?*

I hear them again tonight, Uncle, hard as big brakeshoes,
when I lean over your face in the box of silk. The years
you spent hobbling from room to room alone crawl
up my legs and turn this house to another
house, round and black as defeat, where slugging
comes easy when you whip the gray softball over
the glass diesel globe. Footsteps thump on the stairs
like that fat ball against bricks and when I miss

I hear you warn me to watch the timing, to keep
my eyes on your hand and forget the fence,

hearing also that other voice that keeps me out and away
from you on a day worth playing good ball. Hearing,
Who the hell . . . I see myself, like a burning speck
of cinder come down the hill and through a tunnel
of porches like stands, running on deep ash,
and I give him the finger, whose face still gleams
clear as a B&O headlight, just to make him get up
and chase me into a dream of scoring at your feet.
At Christmas that guard staggered home sobbing,
the thing in his chest tight as a torque wrench.
In the summer I did not have to run and now

who is the one who dreams of a drink as he leans over
tools you kept bright as a first-girl's promise? I
have no one to run from or to, nobody to give
my finger to as I steal his peace. Uncle, the light
bleeds on your gray face like the high barbed-wire
shadows I had to get through and maybe you don't remember
you said to come back, to wait and you'd show me
the right way to take a hard pitch
in the sun that shudders on the ready man. I'm here

though this is a day I did not want to see. In the roundhouse
the rasp and heel-click of compressors is still,
soot lies deep in every greasy fingerprint.
I called you from the pits and you did not come up
and I felt the fear when I stood on the tracks
that are like stars which never lead us
into any kind of light and I don't know who'll
tell me now when the guard sticks his blind snoot

between us: take off and beat the bastard out.
Can you hear him over the yard, grabbing his chest,
cry out, *Who the goddamn hell are you, kid?*

I gave him every name in the book, Uncle, but he caught us
and what good did all those hours of coaching do?
You lie on your back, eyeless forever, and I think
how once I climbed to the top of a diesel and stared
into that gray roundhouse glass where, in anger,
you threw up the ball and made a star
to swear at greater than the Mick ever dreamed.
It has been years but now I know what followed there
every morning the sun came up, not light
but the puffing bad-bellied light of words.

All day I have held your hand, trying to say back that life,
to get under that fence with words I lined
and linked up and steamed into a cold room
where the illusion of hope means skin torn in boxes
of tools. The footsteps come pounding into words
and even the finger I give death is words
that won't let us be what we wanted, each one
chasing and being chased by dreams in a dark place.
Words are all we ever were and they did us
no damn good. Do you hear that?

Do you hear the words that, in oiled gravel, you gave me
when you set my feet in the right stance to swing?
They are coal-hard and they come in wings
and loops like despair not even the Mick
could knock out of this room, words softer
than the centers of hearts in guards or uncles,
words skinned and numbed by too many bricks.

I have had enough of them and bring them back here
where the tick and creak of everything dies
in your tiny starlight and I stand down
on my knees to cry, *Who the hell are you, kid?*

Poems after Wisconsin Death Trip, *by Michael Lesy*

---

1. The Suicide Eater

G. Drinkwine, father of Miss Lillian Drinkwine, who committed
suicide a few days ago, attempted suicide at Sparta. He swallowed a
large quantity of cigar stubs.

Someone came to the door
asking what we are
in this world
for: a religious question,
a sequence of syllables
singsongy really,
not the kind of thing
a man wants to answer
only days after the dirt
of his daughter's going
remains on his boots.
But those sounds whirled
on for days, like sparrows
getting up over here, sitting
down unequivocally somewhere,
and what sense in that?
I watched them many times
from the sun in her room
and no answer. Some
order is all I guessed,
maybe fright. Maybe.

You cannot eat death.
It isn't real, is it?
I called to the stranger.
I was smoking a cigar.
It was real, but it went
out: a plant raised up
in death, then dead
itself, but organized,
useful, its smoke more
tangible than words until
it died. Brown and slimy
and soft in its stink,
I broke it like bread.
Death, like life, creates
its own hunger. I had
to have more, to go on,
to feed. Understandably
there is pain in this,
maybe sickness, but words,
they are the black strangers,
unanswered, inedible.

2. On the Limits of Resurrection

Christ Wold, a farmer near Poskin Lake, committed suicide by
deliberately blowing off his head with dynamite. He placed a quantity
of the explosive in a hole in the ground, laid his head over it and
touched off the fuse exclaiming, "Here I go and the Lord go
with me."

After some years of my clearest testimony
I, for one, remain convinced
that in the readily-available-to the-tactile
senses (barn reek, green moss in blue river ice,
owls like nuns after the copulating cats, etc.)
what speaks plainest is the most mysterious.

My friends in Moss Bones's beer hall (that being
his honest-to-God name) used to go home
with me and I would drag my feet
in the black locust groves
where we had all grown up pricked and bleeding.
My idea was the wind sang the truth there,
fretting the thorns like a fiddler.
If children threw stones at us I said
let them go. One drowned running away.

This year I consumed only cabbage and spring water.
The priest stepped from behind a hedgerow
in December, stinking and thundering
that he was reality (*Look at me,* he shouted. *Look
how my body makes prints in the snow!*) but I
saw beyond his foolishness. I heard owls
blaspheming the language of stones.

One day coming home, I said there is nothing else to do,
I will have to get down among the huddled things
and make a noise to get their attention.
I saw also the only woman I have ever loved
crossing the ridge, visible and silent as a stump.
Then I began to dig and I could hear dear dead mother
padding down the hall, the fat nun knocking
the river riding the bones of that child.

3. Song of the Dutch Insult

Abraham Zweekbaum of the town of Holland committed suicide by
battering himself on the head with a hammer.

First, I found myself kneeling
at the front steps which, blasted by sun,
cracked like the sparrow dung. In need
of fresh paint. I put out my tongue
and missed, striking my nose.
Nose took many smart blows.

Painful, of course, but it did not serve.

So, with my arm and my good hammer,
I struck at my forehead, that harborer
of various offenders. Lifting my arm for fair,
by God I hammered at the gates in the air,
grew moist with sweat, and more.
I opened a door.

My kin will tell you I was not one to swerve.

The day began with a vision over my bed, a glow
perhaps no more than a trick of light,
for I had not slept since I caught
the drifter and my wife, legs and all,
where the blackberries plumped.
Then the bird flew in, wild at my wall.

There are many ways to die and one is in the nerve.

As I have said, the nose went first.
An eye closed, more in sympathy than hurt.
Between the beginning and the end, life
demands forgiveness. I had nailed
a dark thing deeply in. Therefore,
I kneeled to peel the coffin's lid
and prayed to God to save my wife.

4. A Fixation with Birds

Mrs. Anna Ross, a Marquette widow, went insane over religion.
A Chicago revivalist representing Dowie faith healing meetings there
made an attempt to cure Mrs. Ross of lameness. Prayer was tried at
several meetings and the final result of it was insanity for the woman.

The first owl appeared
as the leaves turned,
scarcely a shadow
where I lay in my bed.
The nuns had come, gone,
shaking their heads, my
hell signed and sealed.
I denounced each one,
for they had married
God, though they had
the flesh never rent
by any man. Whereas, so
I swore, I was the bride
bruited for her deeds
of sin, but cleansed, thus
as holy as the rain.
The Baptists agreed.
The Dowie man came.

By winter all the owls
were white with coals
for eyes and talons
pearl-scaled. I told
them of gentle Abraham,
my husband, the blood
we shed that first night.

Without love, how stand
in the wingless world?
The owls cooed for hours.
The Baptists prayed, oh,
they dripped the water,
but in the end went.
Lame, I limped from
wall to wall and named
each owl I nailed up.

Let me not see the spring
come again, I begged.
Veins flamed my legs.
The Dowie man screamed,
"Get thee gone." I did.
Dear Abraham, I cried.
They sealed my doors
and fed me gruel.
Hawks came, and kestrels,
ravens, magpies, crows,
wheeling like fools.
But I was gone, my
wings thickened white.
I ate myself sore
and the world was good.

This is the room where she sickened, the clotted wads of paper.
The smell is that of no-smell or, more precisely, a smell
from the ancestral memory of hair dissolving.

The walls lean down with an absence like an envelope ripped.
The bedsheets lie wrinkled and twisted, but no
blanket, none needed even this near winter.

Someone has left a shoe canted at the dark woodwork, a boot
badly scuffed, its tongue out, no lace.

Only hours ago I stood at these curtains and could not think
what good they did on this poor earth where she slept
in her small frame, where now blade of light
comes in clean and is all

the world offers in its daily deliberations. If we speak of
love, light will answer, *Do you remember me?*

But beyond the light I look, now, parting the gray fabric
whose body and smell are simple things we may know
as we knew the soft last glaze of an eye,

as we know, in time, our own coarse flesh weight and the useless
discarded shape of a shoe, the world's garbage.
We are what the wind moves, scraps of litter
shunted against a fence somewhere, trying

to understand. Or if not that, simply to hold on and know
we are living, now, and nothing else matters. Yet we look
out of our rooms to see the green barn, burned
by wind, the fence diving over familiar hills,

a landscape of lime white in a sun cremating each particular.
We are of these particulars but we do not look
closely enough to know more than what
we have casually touched
until the wind slices
and whatever we leaned on is memory,

is the road I can see from her window, broiling and black,
where the last cars disappear at a mound of earth
under a pale, relaxed sky,

and is also the insatiable lust of the mind to stare down
into a yard where someone stirs a boiling pot
and hogs, snuffling for scraps, blindly
lunge body to body, great scrotums swinging,

their squeals of discovery and pleasure the same
scalded, in dissolution, cries we have made.

Any way you hold them, they hurt.
What's the use, then?

Once in our backyard, by a sparrow's hidden
tremor there in the green wish of spruce,
a full but unfolded body

hung. It bore every color of the world and was sweet
beyond measure. The canyon wind banged
at this then went elsewhere.

Something happened that night.
The sparrow seems to have seen what it was.

Look at him huddled there, mistakably some other shadow,
the sly outlines of his body almost blue as spruce,
the sun like a big wall nearby

and you stepping through it, big, that big
he would almost give up his only wish.

Almost. Almost. Almost.

Isn't this the way hearts beat in the world,
the way pine cones fall in the night
until they don't?

When you pick them up, as children do,
the tiny spot appears in your palm,
red as the sun's first blink
of love.

And that sticking unabidable tar.

Kneeling,
you are without children.
The seeds of the pine
drop on the night wind
and a cry comes your way,
in bent syllables,
over the small lake.
Looking out
from the dark porch
I try to find that
sound you turn to
as if it might swell
the breasts vacantly
you notice each night.

How difficult it is to know
the body that fits each
cry over stilled water,
to know that mouth
sinking under a tongue
of darkness when
something howls
in our dreams. If
we could hear that,
I think, if we could know
even the least gesture
of a seed buoyant
still in wet absence,
we might understand
grace and its song.

The loon, wire-white
as a star streaking,
triggered by reeds,
doesn't mean to grieve,
to cut this moment
with a child's shriek.
He is only trying
to say what he is,
swelling his space
with the news of
the debris he tastes.
Like you he doesn't know
what cry he hears but
goes on answering
in echoed praise
what he could not sing.

I am sitting there with my bitter self-taste,
Lael, Jeddie, Mary, and you asleep overhead
in the blue light I love, that snow wash,
the glass doors locked and iced before me.
If I were not so cold I would go out
into that emptiness to find pure words.
Instead I think of the snow piling up, how
it is like sugar falling through a floor crack
at the foot of a dark mountain, some house
abandoned, the work done, the family gone.
Snow makes its slow statement and I think
of that house, its cold tools and sacked things.
In this way, without flash or any witness,
I have gone down there, a father trying to see
what to do in all this immense swirling. What
I have seen, all night, is the white surge
like a human hand lifted over the dirt
with its own form, its fate, to which
I am nothing watching. I should not stay here.
I should go where words make a clumsy shape
against this heavy drift, where the self
I am can speak its forgiveness in its own
house, in its own tongue. Lifting my eyes
I learn again the shape of your calm faces
and see the snow's light turn them luminous.
Whoever I am, whatever words I badly use,
may we come to the pure heat of our bodies
and keep in ourselves the dark edges
no snow in this world ever softened enough.

Trails of it like trout streaks skid
the Weber River under the scald
of the interstate where swallows
roar past like trucks to build
what winter never remembers.

It has come suddenly, from the mountain,
to glow on the small girl whose hair
flies like feathers from the nest
of her gaze. She is dreaming
what moves inside that flow,

the line in her hand connecting her
to what laps at her hung foot. She
blinks at each dark zooming
of bird, as at a scar still pink
and unbelievable, and I hunch

in my shadow behind her, in slow burning
light that is pure fear, for I
know how greased with quick green
the rocks are, how cold spray
is like a handful of water dropped

from a lover's hand where a girl lies
sunning only for the first deep gaze
up into the dizzying sun, yes, and
the dead-face roll on the back
when memory can resolve nothing,

cannot even give back the face of a man
that somewhere, far upstream, waits.
What is joy but that first squint
of love through hardest light,
and the dreams roaring in futility?

Hours it seems I watch each split twig
fester toward a knot of steel-flaring
water where swallows swoop and take
what they need until at last
I lift my face and know I am

inside the dream no one ever wakes from.
In the terrible light of morning
each bird, each child is a dream
lodged until it slides out
of itself, becoming the vast pouring

dream the world is everywhere. It leans down
from the mountain to dapple the skin
of a small girl like a first peach.
Swallows scream in the air
for the grief of it, and the joy,

and I, seeing her turn up-shoulder to look
into my face, want to warn her.
But what is there to say except
that she must remember this dream
brilliant as a dot of light

in a dark room? Far off on the mountainside
light spears twice and is only a man
on a battered tractor whose
dark face is unimaginable to me
but I squint as if I could see everything.

Under cliffs as ragged as the world's first morning you are
the one who has shucked off the load of ideas that refused
to build a better world, the one who goes hours bent over
in outsized rain gear, hair feathering and bird alert above
sand carved to a crumbling peninsula. Like a grim fugitive
from that exterior world of demands to the east, you tread
the edge of foam and unseen suck of current. I watch you
as if you were a dumb other self, feeling the cold seepage
in that forgotten slit of the boot. That and all else sifts
out through the now darting, now spread net of your hands.
The prospect of so much rubble is overwhelming. Anywhere,

you are thinking, there may be one more perfect than hope,
purple at its heart as a god's gown, blue as a mullet's eye.
It's this that bears you down, fragments that litter thick
in your pockets, a weight to drown you if the sand should
skid or you take a blind step. You won't look anywhere else
until the darkness begins to lock you in. Millions like you,
in any cheap mirror, would feel the emptiness of this place,
would straighten the kinked spine and walk away content with
legs sorely knotted. We know what they say: What good in it?
We agree, there is no cash in what's been heaved up from
the interior, nothing gold but the gold slick of illusions.

The idea, then, is simple and takes you beyond that country
where the telephone is ringing with ancient obligations. I
have watched you enter this dream, if it is a dream, glittering
with the mind's assertive flow. It swirls around delight's
rock, plainly there, and the only need is this final searching.
I have seen this and want to tell you what is going to happen.

The wind will, any moment, come screaming off the ocean
where the last convulsion of sun glowers. Behind you a gaunt
shadow hangs, crippled, ready to follow each step back along
the iced thread of sand. The black suck of the surf will, now,
hammer at your heart. Driving inland each house reminds
you there was someone you loved but never enough, the odd
way walls bow, the black sheen of empty streets. Understand,
too, how so much follows from that first look up into the sun.
It explains why you suddenly jump from your half-sleep where
agates, like someone's eyes, gleam furiously at the darkness.

It blooms in the chokeweed and breathes, turning
the air butternut and blue. A man
climbs the distant horizon, his steps
soundless in the leaves hung
almost reverently, but beginning
to tremble in tune with the first star.

He moves slowly and we are able to turn away while
the stalks of weed sing, while a light flows
from a kitchen window, then find him
as if nothing had changed, as if risen
darkness, like water, brought him
forth on the earth to make us forget ourselves.

Again and again we feel ourselves look away shyly
into the blue thickened behind us,
then back to that shape grown
half visible, and less. We feel
in such light there is no time to waste,

so begin the story that gathers the sweet breath
of our children. It says, *Once upon a time*—
our voice dividing into groans
the wind made that night our father
left the road, our hands parting
the blue air branch after branch as we

wait in a room of light cast on the furred hillside.
Each sound of the cooling earth wants to become
our speech. We hear, we can hardly bear

not to leap up in joy and tears,
but there is only darkness and no one
sliding out of leaves where the world monstrously

gargles its syllables without meaning until we try,
driven red-eyed beyond sleep, to pray.
Calling the names of parents
who were the future and are,
now, the past, we want to fill
the dark with our hands, with ways
a man can get home. Somewhere
there is a path no one can get lost on

until the last hour of the world ends, each small head
lolling in a dream of the infinite undark.
We sink into ourselves as we invent
someone who loves us. He climbs the hill
where the gold has trickled deep blue.
Light from our kitchen falls into his eyes.
Night, giver of morning, comes on, swirling over us.

Amid some moment of grace, unrecognized though the world is
obvious for the most part, joy insinuates itself.
In Salt Lake City I have seen an unremarkable sun
drop behind Antelope Island like a bloodstain
on snow, until the world festered red

and all night, lying in a dark room, felt on each inch of skin
an unaccountable annoyance. The sheet lay on skin
acute, as with an extreme diabetic, until
I kicked it off and was naked
as a boy filling the room with his risen self,

but did not connect my jitters with either sunset or bloodshed
and hardly understand any juncture of eye and memory,
but know the grass everywhere had gone blood-bright
under a cloud-spattered blue sky and know

a swoop of small birds cut a gold scar in what I saw, that silence,
where the world seemed no more than itself. The island lay
ridged against the down-boiling light but was
far west and only shadow in any case,
yet I strained to hear any sound there might be,

and heard the whipping of those small wings, then saw the gold.
And saw one trailing bird shatter in the sudden scar
of the evening hawk that wheeled and was gone.
Saw the wreckage drop into the valley
whose trees reached up like black lake stumps

and my body was rushing with excitement, for I was a young boy
walking home at dusk and my body smelled from the girl
I had loved, finally, and there just over the pine
he lifted at my coming, talons bloodied.

He did not flee, only circled to make that enormous screech
echoing over the river long gold in the last light.
I went on into shadows and stood to see him drop
onto the darkened horizon, but saw nothing
except in the night-long dream and sweat of my joy

where a face, in gold frame of hair, floated, then fell from me.
Her face, years now slipped under the heavy sheet
where what I thought was pain gathered, but this
was only her dark secret, and is now

what I wake with, the whisper of joy kicking to be naked, gold,
silent as the first lips on your neck, gold
where what was blue goes red and bleeds itself empty.

Dream Flights

This book is dedicated to
David Jeddie Smith, Jr.
Lael Cornwell Smith
Mary Catherine Smith

PART I

CRAB

Like other crabs Callinectes sapidus *probably evolved from the oceans.
But it is now an estuarine organism, having found its best place in
life where river and ocean waters blend. What primal drive, then,
impels females to die in their evolutionary cradle? Why are they not
accompanied by males, who are believed to seek out the deepest Bay
channels when their moment comes? And what can we say of the sea
runs who return, befouled and spent, to sample briefly once more the
estuarine gardens of their youth?*
— *William W. Warner,* Beautiful Swimmers: Watermen, Crabs,
   and the Chesapeake Bay

I read once that when he had opened Thomas Wolfe's head,
the surgeon did not even look up,
his fingers needling and cradling
                    back the deep-hidden meat.

The books said postules or nodules, I forget exactly,
and more than once I have caught myself
in the La-Z-Boy, fingertips testing
                    the uneven round of my skull,

and again, then again.
                    They must have been something
gray as bubbles I dream
in the chittering crab teeth
at the bottom of my historical place.

*   *   *

Late summer finds us ready to leave ancient Lake Bonneville,
where the Salt Lake laps the jet runway.

My son thinks of the Little League, my wife
comforts our infant daughter with a vision
of the family waiting, preparing
her for arms that will reach
among many voices
whose Virginia talk is, well,

                              funny!

  *   *   *

I am seated separately with the middle child who is just
six, a stern dreamer like me. She takes time
to walk to the edge of our yard,
singing, remembering,

though she has nothing to remember yet, being six.

She will sit beside me, at the porthole, serene as a clam,
while I describe our country's true geography,
those wiggling rivers that come out in the end
where you always knew they would, her
unfathomable love storing it all,
each fact, guess, bald lie, and jittery joke.

              I like to think about that,
things sinking in, the hand she'll hold
when my knots have finally come to something, as

we sail south.

  *   *   *

The story starts in the DC-10's roar, recurrent, a dream
where a boy ratty-tatty as Huck Finn floats
as if on a tide to a secret spot.
He knows the big crab is there,
on dancing, hardly touching feet.

Yesterday one swipe with the dip net and it was out,
caught, but he turned his back, and crabs
move quicker than jets. Now he'll try again.

*   *   *

I'm prepared to explain how this beauty is hard come by, and do.
The bigger a crab grows the harder to survive
that necessary shuck of the self's house.
He gets tired, sometimes gives up,
but tries to ride the current
home like a familiar dream. The sun calls him.

*   *   *

                                        I dream

a white string dangling in the marsh grass,
my chicken neck ripe.

I've come from the butcher, kind as a man can be,
who shook my small hand. I'm on my way
with a bag full.

My grandmother's sleeping in the dark house
always crackling with fried chicken.
I go in and go out, and do not see her

for the tide is turning. A kid I remember waves from shadows
of the Sisters of Mercy Hospital, his uniform
spanking white, glove slung on his bat.

I don't stop for him. I don't have time.

I seek out the mooring of boats and run when I see
masts sway gently as feelers, run dizzied while bait,
string, bucket, dip net chafe like armor.

Magnolia is white, mulberry red in this fine, soft hour.

In the garage, under the dried droppings of the mud dauber's
generations, we seek the string wound on a stick.
It waits where the walls join, crusted
by skin of moss long hardened
                                        to black flecks.
We cut away the rotted part.
We stretch whatever has some life left
toward the old house where the family chatters gravely.

*   *   *

Look, make this picture for your memory of me, him, who I was!
Learn how doing it right means that climb out
until your face floats in the water, knees hooked
at the borrowed transom, the secret
place.
            See how I bend my neck,
letting sunburn cut deeply in, and clean salt?
We must hear no thing in the world,
breathing inch by inch, paying out the string,
passionately becoming, for all a crab can tell, beautiful swimmers.

*   *   *

Rehearsing in flight the haul of crabs, I talk her through
ways to manage the claws of fear.
                              At six, the mystery's
heart-tugging and true. Already she can see
what's felt along the taut string,
even those festering bubbles,
                              and the place

        deep in my head. It now will be
            remembered right. Loved.

*   *   *

When we come home to the family house, there will be gifts.
There will be painfully drawn, too small faces.
We will wear the sun's stitches and blisters,
the oxide smell of childhood.

She will not divulge where we have been all day crawling
loyal as the tide, then my boy, slumping and homesick,
will lash at her.
            Slowly she will retreat

into this story, her rehearsal of each deep color, touch and claw
I've planted all these long hours. Remembering,
she will inch them all through
everything year after year
going back to crab
where I lived.

            Flying home

she will draw on our dream's power,
on the dark junked corner of the garage
where crabs bubble in thickets of old string,
claws waving as if to receive me at last,

the one who will pay me out all the years just as I was
when she and I were six,
                              burned,

at Grandmother's.

MUD HOLES

For Howard Moss

Only in the heart-given lowering
of a boy's body, a man's if
a boy yet lives in him,
are they seen, and only then
within the live breath that
keeps August's serious weight
drifting over the salt marsh,
for you must go down, out,
into the unexamined field
that is all its great length
profitless, never of wheat
or least grain responsible.
From where you are, it is
a shiver of gold, cropped
hair of a child who once
walked at eye-chance under
the open window of a mother's
kitchen, walked into sun
as pale as that pie crust
she kneaded, or it is an edge
of a rug you have your chin
to, and smells of old dog
asleep, fire crackling near
in its near-blue of water.
In this squat acreage of
cord grass owned by nothing
in the world, there is always
that scut, the ribboned trickle

left by the daydreaming tide,
and around it, on black banks,
the community of holes. They
seem made by no purposeful man,
with a mud-glazed Coke bottle
shoved in, as if to give drink to
the waiting dead in the earth,
but the mud soft as aged skin
keeps nothing of boots or beast's
bulk, only these holes. To have
come here up to your waist
in the whispering creation,
you must walk idly beyond
the garage, the bicycle by
hand painted with stolen
color, and nothing anywhere
ticks slower than this grass.
Then, there you are, as if
you had not, as you have,
taken the dust and gravel
of the home road in memory,
kicking beer cans and bird
bodies worn to thin parchment,
but as if from the other angle,
out of the sea, up the vein
in the heart of the world, all
before you the inexplicable
known that since your birth
has waited. Not to escape,
simply to be here will turn
you face down, will change you
almost to a wing, walking
air and reed tips. Then, up

close, the one bent inside
your body will seem scarcely
to breathe, no question formed
in the gliding jaw, merely
that long look down into holes
having no reason to be there,
as if a great snake had gone
out the other side of himself
without a sound. Nothing
is ever known of the makers
of these, nor of any owners,
nor with any skinned stick
can you cause the slightest
visible movement. If you are
here when water slowly hurls
itself back, you will see
how they take and they hold
like a bamboo flute the notes
no one has played yet, but
might, as you might be more
than you are in pouring sun,
only a shape among shapes
whose moves are as careful
as a crane's raised foot.
At night, years from this way
you have entered, you may find
your eyes effortlessly, slowly
cross the field of a ceiling,
your hand on a woman's breast,
not longing for a thing within
the world, but deep in the world
of your love, knowing at last
everything is here, hearing it

easily fill up like a hall
where the light, cricket steps
of the dead have come to wait.
And it is not that you are held
by any pressure coming down
but by the deeps that wash up,
holy and unpredictable, your own.

ELEGY IN AN ABANDONED BOATYARD

. . . mindful of the unhonored dead
  — Thomas Gray

Here they stood, hour after hour, whom the Kecoughtan believed
gods from another world, one pair of longjohns
each, bad-yellow, knotted with lice,
the godless bandy-legged runts
with ear bit off, or eye gouged,
a fair fight and no fault,

                      who killed and prayed
over whatever flew, squatted, or swam.

In huts hacked from mulberry, pine, and swamp cypress,
they huddled, ripe as hounds.
At cockcrow scratched, shuffled
down sucking marsh paths,
took skiffs and ferried to dead-rise scows,
twenty-footers dutifully designed and of right draft
for oysters, crabs, and croakers.
                        They were seaworthy.

According to diaries hand-scrawled, and terse court records,
our ancestors: barbarous, habitual, Virginians.

Some would not sail, came ashore, walked on the land,
kept faces clenched, lay seed and family,
moved often, and are gone. Of them
this ground says nothing.
                  Of the sea's workmen, not much,

no brass plate of honor, no monument in the square,
no square, merely the wreckage of a place.

But they stood,
proud, surly, black and white
in the morning mist at the hovel of the boatwright,
some thieves, some new married, the hard arm pointed:
Build me one like that yonder!

Meaning
the gray hull I see across the cove,
bottom caved in, canting in the ashen water.

The arm was Daddy's or Granddaddy's, nameless as the hull,
but no need, then, for name, not to the boatwright
hunched in his shadow and bulk. He was known
to crush clams in his scarred palms,
and thus got his payment.
Our kin like as not, he built the derelicts,
snaking trees week-long with the Pap of each
that stood trying to bear his countersunk eyes.

He gave credit to each son,
unless feud intervened in some veiled remark, in which case
spit drawled between the boots,
and took a stick into the great hand,
an awl good as any, to dig
on the earth the grave first line of a keel,

whose broad brow
would sometimes lift seaward, but nothing said,
as the shape buried in memory hove up
and was

changed some, though God knows little enough,
the result, we suppose, of the material weaker than ever,
or creator's whim, that eye-blink,

or a young man's desire to be unlike
the drab hulls he must lie by days out, nights in.
But not too unlike as to start talk.

                    Like that one yonder!

He gave them no image to name change,
and tomorrow was only a best guess,
the sea's habitual story
leaving walls waist-high

                    and rotten as teeth,

leaving the stink of his silence

                    where the hulls riddled.
He had some kind of notion we must labor to forgive,
the fathers feared, shipping us to school in coarse linen,
the message sewn on our chest, with Bible and slate,
where the smart-sounding future was,

                    the world we entered

as blindly as I now have entered his place, feeling
through the back-flung gates of light
for the builder.

I sit at his charred, flood-smoothed log to learn
the lies he allowed each to invent

that he should rise up
to hack out once more
the hill of our future from planks, feeling
joy in my face as he boils pitch and makes ready
to join all. Suddenly I see

                    and take up a cap
left as worthless to hang on a cypress stump,
and fit its stained round to my head.

Merely to wait where the builder heaved shards and chips
and abortive cuts to the tide's tongue-lap
is to feel the unconceived shape
pulse down the arm and into fingers
almost another self's, perfect, enough
to take up a stick
and loose the in-gathered wilderness
of loon, crow, starling, and gull
who cannot believe what they see, but see it,

                          an immense shadow,
on water.
                   Stick in hand, I feel
my eyes harden
            and there it is,
                   the far wind cradle
of the Eagle's wing, hunter now there, now
vanished. I hold my face up
to study how the air heats,
how under him builds the rising funnel,
building steadily myself, but also dreaming change

until I understand, almost, a problem: is he not harnessed,
himself, this light father
designed to sail like a minor god,
to come screeching down to the soft chicks
he will drive off, well fed,
with his lethal, callous-colored talons?

                      Our brothers float and sink,
lovely shadows, by the millions all over the earth.
Putting my back to the one bark-shorn trunk
they have left me, I pull the stick
in the dirt, remembering the long relevance of usage.

                             The line grows

quick with light, with the answering of birds
crying out the only speech they have
for the unfinished country
that looms still,
dreamed, clearer and deeper,
out of the water that seeps,
out of the water that bore us all here.

THE TIRE HANGS IN THE WOODS

For Robert Penn Warren

First it was the secret place where I went to dream, end
of the childhood road, deep-tracked, the dark
behind my best friend's house, blackberry
thickets of darkness, and later
where we stared, with our girls, into the sky.

Past the hedgerow and the house-stolen fields, past
the wing-shooting of crow remembered, I drive
bathed by green dashlight and the sun's
blood glinting on leaves just parted, then see

again the dead end, the dying woods, that stillness still
ticking like throat rattle—and Jesus Christ
look at the beer cans, the traffic, even
hung on a berry vine somebody's rubber,

and wouldn't you know it that tire still hangs.

*   *   *

In the Churchland Baptist Church the hot ivy hung, smelling
of dust, all mouths lifting their black holes
like a tire I kept dreaming. Clenched
by Mother and Father who stank sweetly in sweat,
I sang and sang until the black ceiling
of our house seemed to bellow with storm
and the tire skulled against my eyes
in time with the great clock in the far hall.

Hanging in darkness, like genitals, it made me listen.

*   *   *

Years pass like Poe's pendulum into memory, where I see
one summer night I came to fistfight Jim Jenrett,
whose house she came to and she no more now
than a frail hand on my cheek, and I
am beer-brave and nearly wild with all
the dozen piling from cars. Jesus,
look at us in the ghost flare of headlights,
pissing, taunting, boy-shadows all right,
and me in the tire spinning my childish words.

We pass also, and are blind, into the years like trees
that I cannot see into except to imagine Jim,
dunned by our words, as he goes out
near dawn and steps in the tire
and shies up the electric extension cord, noosed,
by the rope whose tire, burdened, ticks slowly.

*   *   *

Ghost heart of this place, of dreams, I give you a shove
and sure enough I hear the tick and all that was
is, and a girl straightening her skirt walks
smack against you and screams. You know
who laughs, smoking in the dark, don't you?

There are no headlights now, only the arc of blackness
gathering the hung world in its gullet. Blink
and maybe he's there, his great feet jammed

halfway in the hole of your heart,
gone halfway.

*   *   *

Where do they go who once were with us on this dream road,
who flung themselves like seed under berry-
black nights, the faces black-clustered,
who could lean down and tell us
what love is and mercy and why now

I imagine a girl, mouth open in the sexual O, her hair
gone dull as soap scum, the husband grunting
as his fist smacks again, the scream
not out yet, nor the promise
she could never love anyone else.

I climb in the tire, swinging like a secret in the dark
woods surrounded by the home lights of strangers.
She swore she loved me best.

*   *   *

In the church I imagined this place forever behind me
but now I sit here and try to see the road begin.
Blackberries on both sides blackly hang.
Tall trees, in blackness, lean back at me.
When will they come, the headlights washing
over me like revelation, in cars
ticking and swirling?

Once when my mother could not find me, they came here.
He said, "So this is it, the place." It was dark,
or nearly, and she said I might have died.
I asked them what being dead was like.
Like being blind or flying at night.

I shove my foot at the dirt and swing in absolute black.
The whine of the rope is like a distant scream.
I think, so this is it. Really it.

At eighteen, the U.S. Navy eye chart
memorized, reciting what was unseen,
my father enlisted for the duration.
At nineteen he caught a casual wave
wrong off Norfolk, our home, called
Hell by sailors. The landing craft
cast him loose and burst his knee.
He lived, and wore his rigid brace
without complaint, and never in his
life showed anyone his Purple Heart.
I stumbled into that brace and more
when I climbed to our sealed attic
the year a drunk blindsided him
to death in a ditch, and me to worse.

Today I watch my ten-year-old son race
over the slick pages of *Playboy*,
ashamed I brought it home, imagining
his unasked questions have answers.
I remember the chairs I stacked
and climbed, the brace I put on
to see how it felt and, buried
deep in his sea chest, the livid
shapes shoved so far in a slit
of darkness a man could reach them
only hunched, on all fours. I clawed
through families of discharged clothes,
ornaments for Christmas, to feel
the spooky silk of webs slickly
part on my face where blood rushed.

Trussed on their wide bed, my mother lay
surviving wreckage, stitched back
beyond the secrets I knew he kept.
I shimmied through a dark hole
in the ceiling and listened to pine
rake the roof like a man's shuffle.
But he was dead and the box unlocked.
His flashlight pulsed through my body,
each glossy pose burning my eyes
that knew only airbrush innocence.
Sex rose in me like a first beard.
A woman with painted nails peeled
a foreskin, another held a man
kingly rigid at her tongue's tip.
I could not catch my breath.

I blinked at one spread on a table covered
by lace grandmotherly clean and white.
Here might have been service for tea,
dainty cups, bread, a butter dish,
except she was in their place, clearly
young in middy suit. Behind her a vase
of daisies loomed, the parlor wall
held *Home, Sweet Home* in needlepoint,
and curtains were luminous at a window.
I remember the eyes, direct and flat,
as if she had died. Girlish stockings
knuckled at her knees, her plain skirt
neatly rolled. The man, in Victorian
suit, cradled her calves in furred hands,
and looked at the window, placid as
a navigator. He cut her like a knife.

After school, at night, weekend afternoons,
I raced to see them do it, legs cramped
in that freezing slot of darkness, gone
wobbly as a sailor into the country.
I came and went in the black tube,
ashamed, rooting like a hog to see.
In one sequence a black man held a pool
cue to a white woman, a black woman
held in both hands white and black balls.
The uniforms of sailors were scattered,
wadded everywhere I looked. I smelled
the mothballs from my father's chest
when late at night I woke to vomit
and stare at a clock's one-eyed glow.

How long does it go on, the throbbing dream,
waking obsessed with a hole in the air?
In Norfolk, from loaded cars, we spilled
at sailors passing alleys, asking where
we'd find some girls, beer, a good time.
All answers were sucker-punched. *Bye-bye,
Seafood*, we screamed, then headed down
toward the Gaiety Theater and whores
bright as moths. We spit at mothers who
yelled, *Fuck you kid!* They never would.
The secrets of our fathers, we cruised
the hopeless streets blank as razors,
remembering nothing but naked images
whose neon flared like pus. Seeing now
my son bent to see I imagine at last

my father climbing before me in blackness,
with the tiny light a man carries, bent

on pained knees where I will kneel also
at nameless images we each live to love
and fear. One is a young Spanish dancer
whose crinolines flare out around her
hidden rose. Another cooks in high heels.
Among these are angels, blonde sisters,
classmates suddenly gone from our towns,
one on a patio reclined, her long leg
crooked in invitation. She does not hide
the shorter leg. Each grins and burns
into our memory, speaking in shy whispers,
who are born to teach us violations.
At eighteen what fathers teach is wrong,
for the world is wrong, and only women
know why, their eyes dark and flat.

It isn't eyes that sons remember, blinded
by what never lies or leaves, but
sun's glint on that raw breast, that
thigh where face should not be but is,
and is the curve of the world's flesh
radiant in its rottenness, the secret
that leaves, finally apart and other,
all who walk on the earth. In memory
I see how each breast, each leg, each
face hissed our shame. By accident
I became the boy-father of the house,
owner of obscenities and a family
of creeps who fingered me as one.
What else is the world but a box,
false-bottomed, where the ugly truths
wait sailing in the skins of ancestors?

Escaping them at last I left for college.
But first climbed to what he left me,
carted that box and brace to grave,
and spilled those mild faces down
under the looming Baptist spire.
I spread gasoline where he lay, then
with his navy Zippo snapped it off.
Quick bodies coiled and flamed, ash
flecks disappearing in sun forever.
I gouged the remains in a trench
of churchly dirt, tried once to spit,
then turned in the dark to catch a bus.
His pea coat was black as the sea
at midnight but I took it and wore it,
sweating against the cold to come.

Women smiled at me as if I'd been flush
with cash from months at sea. *Welcome,*
Swabby, one said, *you can sit here.*
I was free, I thought, discharged from
Hell into the world that, for Christ's
sake, waited. I left home in a wink.
And would not go back at Christmas,
being after all busy, being holed up
with the nameless girl, the long blade
of her body even now slicing memory,
that darling who took my coat. But
by Easter was ready, went. House sold,
Mother gone, maybe married, maybe Florida,
they said. I wandered in a cold sea wind,
almost on shore leave, until I came
cast up where my father lay. Posters

of the nailed Jesus littered the grass,
announcing our inexplicable life. I saw
the crones kneeled there in sunbursts,
faceless, soft, as if to serve the sun
dying in the background. I shivered,
then rose up, hearing traffic hiss,
and walked until I found the old road.
I wished I had our goddamn stolen coat.
Boys yelled at me, but no one stopped.
Freed, I was myself. Who understands?
I walked hours in hard places, into night,
my first beard tingling, dreaming what
fathers know. I came to a seedy house.
Among sailors I, a man, heard the siren
call us forward to sit with the darkness
under reels of lighted, loving women
in the theater called Art's House.
At love's edge, braced, we were nineteen.

So we went in.

That year the war went on, nameless, somewhere,
but I felt no war in my heart,
not even the shotgun's ba-bam
at the brown blur of quail.
I abandoned brothers and fathers,
the slow march through marsh
and soybean nap where
at field's end the black shacks
noiselessly squatted under strings
of smoke. I wore flags of pink:
shirts, cuff links, belt, stitching.
Black pants noosed my ankles
into scuffed buck shoes.
I whistled "Be-Bop-a-Lula"
below a hat like Gene Vincent's.
My uniform for the light, and girls.

Or one girl, anyway, whose name I licked
like candy, for it was deliciously
pink as her sweater. Celia,
slow, drawling, and honey-haired,
whose lips hold in the deep mind
our malignant innocence, joy,
and the white scar of being.
Among my children, on the first
of October, I sit for supper,
feet bare, tongue numb with smoke,
to help them sort out my history's
hysterical photographs. In pink

hands they take us up, fearless,
as we are funny and otherworldly.

Just beyond our sill two late hummingbirds,
black and white, fight for the feeder's
red, time-stalled one drop.
They dart in, drink, are gone,
and small hands part before me
an age of look-alikes, images
in time like a truce wall
I stare over. The hot, warping
smell of concrete comes, fear
bitter as tear gas rakes
a public parking lot. "Midtown
Shopping Center, Portsmouth, Va.,"
the *Life* caption says, ink
faded only slightly, paper yellowing.

Everyone is here, centered, in horror
like Lee Oswald's stunned Ranger.
A 1958 Ford Victoria, finned,
top down and furred dice hung,
seems ready to leap in the background.
The black teenager, no name given,
glares at the lens in distraction.
Half-crouched, he shows no teeth,
is shirtless, finely muscled,
his arms extended like wings.
White sneakers with red stars
make him pigeon-toed, alert.
His fingers spread by his thighs
like Wilt Chamberlain trying
to know what moves and not look.

Three girls lean behind him, *Norcom H.S.*
stenciled on one who wears a circle
pin, another a ring and chain.
Their soft chocolate faces appear
glazed, cheeks like Almond Joys.
They face the other side, white,
reared the opposite direction,
barbered heads, ears, necks.
In between, a new shiny hammer
towers like an icon lifted
to its highest trajectory.
A Klan ring sinks into flesh,
third finger, left hand,
cuddling the hammer handle.
This man's shirt is white, soiled,
eagle-shaped, and voluminous. Collar up.

Each detail enters my eye like grit
from long nights without sleep.
I might have been this man, risen,
a small-town hero gone gimpy
with hatred of anyone's black eyes.
I watch the hummingbirds feint
and watch my children dismiss them,
focusing hammer and then a woman
tattooed under the man's scarred
and hairless forearm. The scroll
beneath the woman says *Freedom.*
Above her head, in dark letters
shaped like a school name on
my son's team jacket: *Seoul, 1954.*
When our youngest asks, I try

to answer: A soldier, a war . . .
"Was that black man the enemy?"

I watch the feeder's tiny eye-round
drop, perfect as a breast
under the sweater of a girl
I saw go down, scuttling
like a crab, low, hands no use
against whatever had come to beat
into her silky black curls.
Her eyes were like quick birds
when the hammer nailed
her boyfriend's skull. Sick,
she flew against Penny's wall,
our hands trying to slap her sane.
In the Smarte Shop, acidly,
the mannequins smiled
in disbelief. Then I was
yanked from the light, a door

opened. I fell, as in memory I fall
to a time before that time.
Celia and I had gone to a field,
blanket spread, church done,
no one to see, no one expected.
But the black shack door opened,
the man who'd been wordless,
always, spoke, his words intimate
as a brother's, but banging out.
He grinned, he laughed, he wouldn't
stop. I damned his lippy face
but too late. He wiggled

his way inside my head.
He looked out, kept looking
from car window, school mirror,
from face black and tongue
pink as the clothes we wore.

Often enough Celia shrieked for joy,
no place too strange or obscene
for her, a child of the South,
manic for the black inside.
When he fell, she squeezed
my hand and more, her lips came
fragrant at my ear. I see them
near my face, past the hammer.
But what do they say? Why, now,
do I feel the in-suck of breath
as I begin to run—and from her?
Children, I lived there and wish
I could tell you this is only
a moment fading and long past.

But in Richmond, Charlotte, God knows
where else, by the ninth green,
at the end of a flagstone pathway
under pine shadow, a Buick waits
and I wait, heart hammering,
bearing the done and the undone,
unforgiven, wondering in what
year, in what terrible hour,
the summons will at last come.
That elegant card in the hand
below the seamless, sealed face—
when it calls whoever I am

will I stand for once and not run?
Or be whistled back, what I was, hers?

In Utah, supper waiting, I watch my son
slip off, jacketed, time, place,
ancestors of no consequence to him,
no more than pictures a man carries
(unless a dunk shot inscribed).
For him, we are the irrelevance of age.
Who, then, will tell him of wars,
of faces that gather in his face
like shadows? For Christ's sake
look, I call to him, or you will
have to wait, somewhere, with us.
There I am, nearest the stranger
whose hammer moves quicker
than the Lord's own hand. I am
only seventeen. I don't smoke.
That's my friend Celia kissing me.
We don't know what we're doing.
We're wearing pink and black.
She's dead now, I think.

She could not come here, among these cruising
sons, among the gray gape mouths
that pass with the old songs
spilled into the easy air.
I watch them relentlessly look
for the girl whose grin
bleeds in their taillights.
Being black she could not
come here that summer, but did,
and sings near me from wrecks
resurrected to glide under
the Buckroe Pavilion's lights.
Childbearing horses gallop here
and a calliope's nightmare pumps on.

*   *   *

Obsessive as the sea, she slipped past the cop.
Tonight I am washed back to our common
ground, through the black shacks
along the dead's road, and I look
for love's ageless child,
Celia, the Queen Street stepper,
beautiful mother of moonlight.
Once, years ago, I saw the brute
blue arm reach out and rip free
her brown breast that light made
finely gold, and white faces
sang *Nigger!* Glass-bright, yet,

as glass, brittle, she broke
through a line like this one, passing.

*   *   *

For hours they wheel, the black line in the light
scattered from horses that pump
without expression. Some drop out
to lie by bulkheads in twos
and some are saddled in back seats.
In the dark almost I see them
gone speechless as the dead,
spent in the world's grit.
She trembles there, nameless.
It is night and night's business
is under way, and she has come
ghostly where once I saw her hang
above the seawall, stringing spit
down on my girl's wide screaming face.

*   *   *

Nigger! we screamed, but, ghost-quick, she
lost us. I remember that wall,
those who rose buck-assed from love
of a night's hunt, and I find
                              myself twenty
years later still dreaming
we roared toward Phoebus and words
I hear hissed in the night, half-
howled like pieces of song. They
nick me like small knives

she could not escape, stuttering
Celia, Celia under the moon.
Down Queen Street we ran her
and caught her and put her under the pines.

*   *   *

Who does a man beg for his life when song
comes heart-drumming and a name
shakes back the sea inside?
We lay her down on the bitter bed
of needles, who rose flat-browed.
I went in the world, cruising,
and scattered myself in words
but could not hide and heard
her call, as those now hear
the silence and the gull screech.
We come Celia, we are pitched
among the undying as if hope
might come here and step out
free, dancing, true, and our own.

*   *   *

I sit and watch them pass through sea whine
and star trickle. Their faces go
around dappled and I think
of sleet spitting in D.C.
where my name once was
called. It was you, speaking
from a slit in the soft night,
dazzling and golden, drawing me down.
But I ran, I hid out in Utah, not

expecting to come round a corner
where your breath needled the air.
She's long dead, I thought, a man's
got a right to believe that at least?

*   *   *

Why won't you stay in a stinking room I remember
filled with the cruiser's blue light?
Cops came, one black, one white,
batons swinging, badges like moons,
spit-shined boots on stairs like time.
Her name? Celia, the old one, back
again, cleaned me, I said, and what about
the law? Somebody has to find her.
Ur-white grinned, *Yeah, so what, craphead?*
Well, she looked near dead, only . . .
Only? The black one now, giggling,
baton in my chest,
                    This Niggertown,
boy. She gone, and you better run.

*   *   *

She could not come here, I think, running
in my head where the calliope pumps
and the thousands of needles
of light leap into faces
that pass where I sit, waiting.
If only I could hear the songs
each follows I think I might know,
unspeakable nightmare of love,
where you are, what you want.

These are my brothers. We summon
you sweet ghost face, glass body,
yourself, life wind, shadow,
keeper and queen of night's business.
We wait like children to rise up with you.

PART 2

ARTIFICIAL NIGGERS

For Primus St. John

How do you expect me to know anything when
you don't tell me right.
—Flannery O'Connor, "The Artificial Nigger"

We're gathered behind my grandparents'
goldfish pond, two boys flanking
the smaller girl. She's gray,
fidgeting as the Kodak snaps.
Her hand, making a fist, rises
as if about to strike one of us.
He is black and I am white.
We are frozen in this moment
of our famous southern grins.

* * *

Once each year I go down into dust
and pull these photographs out.
Among children I watch
how the images gather themselves
into the history of our kind.
For hours we are buried,
inventing the ground, the air,
the silence that cannot speak
except in the small human voice,
never well enough heard,
singing out of the head's light
and dark memory of its place.

That water you see is the black James,
the land is Virginia, our green dream.

*   *   *

Before the three of us, in foreground,
the little pool, maybe six feet
across, bears the sun's ripple
straight as a good rope.
Our dead built it to keep
tame fish outside but near.
Note how lilies lean, tall,
yet stooped. They will break
rocks with roots black and deep.

*   *   *

We weren't allowed to play with goldfish
or lilies, but I stood over them
on that bridge long as a boy
and saw the artificial nigger
loom at the pond's heart.
His lantern cast a shadow
like time toward the southern
edge of the frame he stares from.

*   *   *

My mother snapped these "cute" shots
from the dark house. She called
but I would not leave my friends.
We stood in the red dusk, crabs
we caught that day hissing

from a basket behind us.
Claws locked in a fearful
chain, some smothered,
some ripped themselves apart.

*   *   *

The basket makes a dark sort of moon.
Our gray girl waits, eyes wide
over the head and red hat
of the artificial nigger.
Wind and years of grins
chipped his face to plaster.
He seems to look for himself inside.

Mother's next shot, through a window,
catches all of us bent over,
faces in the basket, bottoms
stained with local mud.
Legs and arms we are fused
by the camera, an odd growth
of the unseen crabs. Shadows
stretch thin. Soon we will divide.

*   *   *

But not before the incident singing
wordless as a sting in my head.
This print is blurred. Two boys
and one nigger locked, each
pushing at the other. Then,
amazed, on that bridge,
we look into the headless

figure. A slight smoke
grayly spirals between us.
The red cap sinks invisibly.
Wasps by the hundreds are rising.

Next, the basket is tipped on its side.
The crabs run and hide. I lie
by the pond stones, face down.
Dots or speckles cover my shirt,
my hands, my exposed neck.

The black boy, accused, has fled.
Our girl, centered, holds me
down, her fist in mid-air.
Her smooth chest shines
except for some tiny knots.
Her face is wizened, dark,
and it screams.

*   *   *

I was then near school, the fall coming,
and I lay in bed as storm gathered.
My room went black, then white
as leaves clawed and tore loose.
Half-dreaming, I heard "niggers"—
and mother somewhere said
this place had gone to hell,
our father at war, we must
run or lie down and be buried.
Now I wake in another country,
remembering that lilied ground.

We look at the pictures as if they were
dreams running. In one a black girl
sits on the steps of our house.
We have gone back. She waits
for someone to let her inside.
I took her picture but can't
find it among so many. How
could you live in my house
and me in yours? she asked.
It was hot and quiet, the air
smelled of rotting crabs.
She took us to see the pond
where no fish swam. Sometimes,
she said, I dream they are
all in the air, me too,
just going around, black and white.

With White Hair, They Come

And are always suddenly there, the knock on glass
polite, formal, a man retired, teeth gold inlay.
Three raps, in the old manner. Stiff, courteous,

the pink flesh, wide-pored, stands in the porch shade
as it did, doubtless, for her who waited on staircase
to spiral down slowly. The black coat's threads

hang under the coiling white hair and a light grease
of sweat lies on the lip. The cane shuffles backward.
He recalls no name, says: "Sir, could you call please—

for someone is expected." That moment again, awkward
and familiar, his red, mad, extended palm offering
its delusion. Forced to it, you repeat, "Sir, no card

lies in your hand. No one waits. There is nothing
to be done." And him, "Sir, is she under the willow?"
Trembling now, his white hair loose. The ring?

Someone was expected, there had been a ring and "Oh, you
see there was a misunderstanding . . ." And here
the hand falters, retreats, the sun through magnolia

lays down a sizzling tunnel and he passes out where
in he came, in dust dazed, and his leg, lame,
audibly drags like time. He returns every summer,

lingering like a scent at dusk in the yard. Tenant,
like him, you will forget the sun, the dark,
but the last time you were loved always asks you in.

Young Woman, Your Name Is Known

Or else he does not rise from the wickered rocker
in which, in this memory, the hard eyes
glitter and pour forth in passion, as if a river

seen once is always seen, as if yours are her thighs
gone nakedly long in the sun. That first
chance of love leaps back to his breath and cries,

for your skirt is discreetly stained. Sometimes his hurt
glance follows you down the street,
and the light glows on him hot as youth or art.

If he should speak now? But he never quite does that.
In this memory it is also near dusk.
He is your tenant, your ancestor, an edge of fate

where you garden in cool dirt. Unearthing rust,
spoons blackened, some silver, you pat
your hair as she must have, the sweat on your breasts

tickling a little, then you listen. Where he sits
most days the awning is curled in tight.
What makes that rocker rock when there is no wind?

Dammit he's gone again, calling Celia, who is dead
or long gone, and not you, whoever she may be,
though he imagines you are her and asks you to bed.

Maybe he's near, like a child, saw something fleet,
a bird, say, and has gone leaving that murmur
of absence you've suddenly noticed. Or it might be

he's watching you, has been, from a stand of pine where,
white-haired, sick, he whimpers, "Celia,
oh, Celia." Or hides and is trying to comb his hair.

Because you are a woman whose heart was right-raised,
you rise and go seek him out, who knows
how a lady takes time. Go then, but scarcely in haste.

Azaleas

Such flowers have grown long in Virginia, perhaps
elsewhere. No one picks them except icy March.
The month that there is always the sea and salt

and wave-wide horizons and the scented bitter season
she's learned to fear. And today is nail-sudden
on her white parlor wall where a whiter absence is.

She can see, almost, the neap tide and far bells ring.
She recalls how little she knew of a man
loved in his madness, without pride. Her life is long,

is sitting in this room, ash-acrid, and counting failures
that are only the heart oozing like firestones,
her window wind-raked with first buds of azaleas.

Bits of paper tremble, some knickknacks of history
made for children of neighbors, of torn news,
but suddenly she stiffens for knock at door, as if he—

and remembers oiled slate hauled from County Fluvana:
her father's bride-gift, dark stones, and wicker
chairs for summer. How light danced on that veranda

when she was swept up, comically, and scrubbed in whiskers!
Footsteps sound on slate up to the door.
Afraid, she leans far forward, the steps disappear.

If now they should come again, his steps and his knock
blunt on opaque glass, oh, azaleas must litter
the hard ground with small beauties, and a black

pain come at the heart like the nail that surprises
with its sharp shiny thrust out of the wall. She
whispers the name of one whose picture hung in whiteness

before the world seemed only salted nights and debris.
Her fingers are old. He did not return
from whatever war he had attended and now she,

who understood nothing of blooded azaleas or tide's urge,
mountain-born, sits and is rootless and hopes
for something as yet unimagined, or ever remembered.

The children will come soon. They'll knock on her door.
They don't know her name, but he did. He did!
And what does this paper mean, like hair, on the floor?

In her hand the knife, brisk, brilliant as moon claw,
shaves the flesh. It grazes the white
belly just over the heart.
Underneath, the coiled fingers
are cradling a soft flesh
as if it were the jowls of the aged

man propped for awhile on the bench in the park.
The head is not severed, the eyes not out.
Blue, they appear to flash odd ways
where a tree makes a live shadow.
Mostly the eyes are dead.
Nothing is in them

except the intense blue of sky the tree allows.
There is no conspiring of nerves,
no least event recalled
by a limb's high arching,
or even a girl's ascension
from a forgotten distance of water.

But there is something as she lifts the meat.
It is enough to draw down her gaze.
Now her arm rises against
yellow hair fallen
white in a childish face.
She is still as a leaf barely clinging.

I come to her like a cat in the stunned grass
and touch her to see the startled
up-thrusted gleam of her face.
At brow and each cheek
like gathered beads of mist
scales leap with the sun, and are dead.

No word passes between us, but something electric
as a flash of steel makes her
cry out just once. Squatting
at the yard's edge, she
sings beyond any thought.
Her knife flies as lethal as love
and cuts quickly in like a hurried kiss.

We called it love's house and it was plain
by that creek where the tidal
changes were ordinary,

though once, Celia, we heard the cry there
of a beast's looming,
and did not know what had happened.

The cry comes
keening still out of the water-buried
acres of distance when I touch you.

But sometimes I wake in memory's
half-sight in the dark room of fear, and all
is
      vanished.

*   *   *

              Night-long,

before the twining of our bodies had ended,
we heard the mares drumming the earth
along the frailest spirit of fence.

The stallion far off kept himself
saddled in mist, head down in a field
he commanded alone. We heard how they called him.

Hoof strikings knocked late at the edges of our sleep.

* * *

         Vanished, that out-of-the-world place
swells in my head and reveals
a moment waking sweat-glazed in love.
A man, thick and sluggish
with joy, hears, stands,
              blinks,
listens before the sun. Is me.
              Is.

* * *

With you I saw how the world could drown.
A live skin of water tidally risen
now rippled around love's house.
No walkable ground was there.

            Something cried out. I saw,

standing in that timeless blue running,
one who had gone apart from others,
whose hooves held the ground
only a few inches deep,
              one borne
almost wholly by the darkness of water.

* * *

Her head merely was shining in first light
as if she came out of a deep-wombed
world we had not known.

And made then that summoning cry
for all that would vanish
to be seen again, and not ordinary at all ever.

And stood there so I thought she was
composed of sun fleck entirely,
that motionless spirit of power

I found in the house of your love.

*   *   *

                    Alone, like a fervent secret of water,
she stood, her one sufficient note given.
I felt one far off lift his head
where something like a thought
of ice already ran,

and felt how under her hidden body
each fish and crab looked up
in astonishment,
as if all was about to vanish.

*   *   *

When I think of this moment I want to fall deeper
into the sleeping love that holds all
houses alive, to conceive

words in which men and women are summoned
to cradle themselves exactly right
against the neap
of dark.

I remember the water horse unshakably moored, unable
to leap from one world to another,
bearing the essence of both,
over the voided country,

like the image of your face
in my memory, and I saw at once

a house we could live in endlessly,
and the ordinary redemption that is passion.

*   *   *

Hoof striker,

I remember that dawn
when wide water fell down.
Many mares were lining the shore,

but one stood a little way off, waiting.
I saw how you went in.
Together two rose,
silted and shaggy, glistening.

All followed and went into the field
and there ate the misted grass
without fear, having seen

the ordinary turning of water
she commanded, you obeyed,
as if nothing had changed,

as if the world were only a place
always about to vanish, as it is
without the one summoning song of love.

THE TRAVELING PHOTOGRAPHER: CIRCA 1880

For A.G., in memoriam

Everything about him must be conjectured, his life
whatever a man's life is, succession of moments
under pine, catalpa, sedge, his sour
shirts, habitual horse, creaking wagon.

He takes no portraits of himself, on principle.
Yet, lying dreamless in the hot night, knows
it is all there, in plates
stacked, a joke no one learns the end of.

He laughs, and wind in the harness bell laughs.
Where, how did this life begin?
The plopping sound of the mare
makes him wish he could capture the night.

So much lost in black. He smells himself,
the heaving desert, and oddly
a wedge of butterscotch cake.
His mother, serving him, had laughed.
Son, go far. Dying.

Yes, *far.* The laugh, now,
burrs in his throat, but he remains
hungry, salivating at the ebb of his fire.

Closing his eyes, eyelids develop a cargo
of images (it is all there), the longing,
corn cakes, people, grubby people, their towns,

bluebonnet somewhere, stream, a snake weaving dust,
his wheels crossed it, the plate all
the evidence he was there.

Each thing is itself always, arcane
in the wagon, a junction without voice, theory, or
connection except the chuckhole's incessant clink-clink.

So little in all the world, monstrous
stars like a blacksmith's steel burning back the hoop
of his out-of-rounds wheels. The night trembles
like mountain water, aching his teeth.

Well, he will die soon enough.
He tries to remember an orchard at Shiloh,
sees instead the last plates stacked, is
nevertheless aware

his belly, too, prints the fishbone of his back.

*   *   *

Cat squall, wolves, red-eye have been companions.
From the fire and from the glassy darkness
they leap like old friends. He is
somewhere west of Denver, mountains
black that had been green as fresh buffalo chips.

In dust before the trading post, patting his horse,
he had been ready to move on, had taken
all day two plates, bartering.
The whore was not worth it.

The minister who repaired cabinets
fixed his wagon to shut as it ought to.

At his elbow the child's hand, the laboring breath.

* * *

They were waiting, still in the usual way.
He could not tell them from a thousand others scattered,
cinders of a prairie fire.
Father and mother centered, grandfather, sleeve pinned up,
children like stairs, too many.
Seat the smallest in the dirt, let them
have legs crossed.

Dead in the middle, in tiny coffin, the laced burden
upright against the sod door. Stitching,
fine red and green thread blossoms
on its tiny nightgown.

Color won't show, nor hours of work nor
the idle chatter before powder's explosions.
How did it happen? Name and age of the child? Well, God's

will be done. Wait for the wind
hotly swirling, and always long for a quick shot
of whiskey, for Christ's sake.
The nightgown had blown up, her flesh all sunk, sallow,
backbone, surely, clear as a fish in shale.
Made two more plates.

Hours riding into dusk toward fire flare and night,
he spits what flew under his hood,
spits, but it is still there.

His father, the circuit rider, had condemned him
for those "damn pitchers" and burst himself
in clots on his mother's pillow.
Smoke from the campfire wavers like a face.

*   *   *

Had he had some kind of calling, a mission? What?
Night lowers itself at him again,
red-eye, and the eerie blue of full moon.

At the stream's place, his image wobbles up at him.
The mare now and again lifts
its peaceable muzzle
to whicker whatever it whickers.

Things happen, things are. That's all.
Who has moved in the world more than he has,
gone farther, to know less?

Sometimes with his face splashed clean, flat on his back
between the stacked rows of glass plates,
the faces, unlost, try to speak.
He listens

until sleep comes, or dawn.
Sometimes their stories transform his own life,
strangers, nameless, become his father, his mother,
offering him children he calls Amelia and Darce.

Night-long they wheeze, electric as rattlesnake rattle.
Always with the first cluck to his horse
they are only themselves,
slabs of glass clinking behind him.

He has tried to be himself with poor luck.

*   *   *

Months into the wilderness, wheels busted again, fixed again,
pain like a broken tooth comes
in the middle of his chest.
Waking in dead heat, his shop is cottonwood shade.
Late afternoon, the last plates prepared,
what does it matter?
Why hurry to have it all completed?

Works steadily, feeling fat, sore. Is it an illusion?

Held up to the sun, the glacial doll rivets him,
her eyes open, black holes gone red
as star-burn or wolves. Tilts it, then
again, and yes he has her
off-center, goddammit.

Sits down plop on the baked dirt, and stares. Stares,
then hurls the plate to shatter on dung-colored rocks.

"Longinus, we made mistakes but we tried."
The horse, at its name, blusters
head down in witchy green.

*   *   *

The artist wakes dry-mouthed, unaware he had fallen asleep.
In late, brilliant sun, he lifts
the second plate close to his brow.
Head and body, he is rock-cradled.

The father, long-armed as an ape taken in Kansas City,
holds an apple hugely bitten.
He had not seen this.

Now sees. Squints,
lets it fall onto his face.
Feels the clench of his belly.
The seepage of saliva comes thickly.

Tries to spit, but cannot
force a thing to move, knows he is

hungry.
Eyes widening,
seeing as whole families do
into orange wolf-gleam of the sun,

he feels himself draining too quickly, blackness,
and fire sparks flying over ordinary ground
where all is ash, smoldering.

His wagon looms like one chance
for unity, brittle hope,
one last image

blurred,

near
and just so far.

Crackling like fear in the child's heart late awakened,
the parents have gone into nightmare,
on the night lake of darkness
far away are carried, and the house
dreadfully closes.

It smiles like dawn in the wide western window.
No one believes this ever.
But there is glass-flutter.

There is wind hungering and the far sister
of the aspen trying to crawl.

Then it will be seen to leap the ridge distance,
going entirely.
Something has come in the dark, touching.
But the air wonderfully now

is sheepish and light lacquers all.

Snow light nearly, down,
the singlet of geese travelers,
something like a word from the North,

this wholeness fully breathable
heaping its handful of gray on the ground.
Like mist and fog from a mill town rising
as if the earth had been just
created,

as it has,

and memory's hand opening above the coverlet,
and the family mouth open
and all over.

Packing to move, I unearth something swaddled and heavy,
my grandfather's Winchester pump, Model 12, stock
sheenless and smoothed by a family of hands,
the smell I would know in any dark
of closet or crypt, its great
boom and yellow lick of delight
lashing the canopied undershadow of woods
while morning's blue trickled October dawn.

We sat on the log. Eleven squirrels once. Eleven times
he stood and at noon his bag-coat hung, seams
seeping from small bodies he carried.
Mine then was the .22, short-barreled
clicker, now on my son's wall.
It was as new as I was, sharp-
sighted, never fired,
but right-sized, at any event, for pretending.

At the stream we must cross that cold day he pointed,
then spread his palm on twelve gold cartridges.
Six shots high, the red woodpecker
stoically waited. Then five times
he climbed up the wounded trunk
and turned on me the dark eye that said, *No score.* Yet.

*   *   *

Going home in his vaulted Hudson, the James River gray
rocking below, I watched oystermen tonging in red
baseball caps, their motions like applause.

Wordless as a log, he stared ahead.
Later, his hands dried, rough,
he held out the pail with pink
chips of flesh rising and falling. And eleven shapes.

"Remember," he said. Did he mean his careful, least gestures?
Those gutted entrails that bore blue
shadows amid the bloodied water?
Pumping the breech so it clanged open,
he held the channel for me to look.
From far down the sweet oil rose
like pine sap at autumn's end glazing
the bright hollow, spotting our ancestral stock.

*　*　*

At the window, wrapped in Grandfather's stained coat, I lift
the family gun and break it open. My son,
eleven, obliviously climbs a tree.
Aiming beyond him toward home,
I remember that woodpecker,
its odd knowledge, the way
it flared with lazy yellow wings
into the dark that spread in my body,
and the lashing smell of the Model 12 in a white
room where old eyes scissored, cut for me, and waited.

Hawaii to Salt Lake City

Mid-January, leaving Honolulu, we are all tanned and strange
      with our secrets tucked away
under seats. Pillows spill from overhead. We lean into them,
      as into clouds, and safely
sail past Pearl Harbor, a submarine and wake clear below

but inexplicable as history or even our mute, cramped
      selves. Over coral and mild miles of
sea-dreaming, I wonder how men and women survive and
      explain this world so vastly lavish.
Who are we, so constant in our going down, our rising up,

what news do we cart through the void above the cruising
      unbreakable shadow of our United
hunchback? We feel in its low roar we can climb above all,
      do, and light is shattering.
Many watch movies between worlds, but some glide in thought,

in the hiss of space where nothing is known except the
      selves who sit, exiles of speech, humps
of flesh and fear and hope, unable for a long time to alight.
      We see no streetlights, cars, roads,
no hills, no bowl of star houses to remind us of anyone's life

in the home we dream. Great fish, down there, nose through
        whatever falls on a wind
of water. In their lives there is nothing unremembered or
        known. They go no place in love
or joy. If there is a shadow they enter it and become it

without fear, without knowledge that what they are always
        in is themselves, that harmony.
Dreaming of fish, I drift, I imagine the loved ones we fly to,
        the car that is waiting, soft
questions from runway to house. They do not want our secrets

exactly, only what we have bagged and brought back, gifts
        for children, what may be kept
from that other, illusory world. Coming home half asleep, I
        remember faces I have left,
and left before, their quick eyes in love with whatever rises

out of a place not even dreamed, a word only, like sunlight.
        Yet somehow I feel, floating,
I have become a bad gene they already harbor without
        knowing. Mid-sea, ungrounded, I see
the plane move backward to start over. Snow smothers the peaks

of Utah, home valleys dark as the volcano on the big island
        of Hawaii where I have not yet
gone. Houses sunk and dormant seem to erupt in the black.
        I stand at my child's window,
3 A.M., shadowy as a shark, from home light about to fly far

over the black bottomland that once was ancient Lake
      Bonneville. Newspapers say the Salt Lake is
rising, the airport will go first, flood crest only one, maybe
      two thousand years off. Our
houses will become the spewn gray mist. I feel in my body

bodiless ancestors claw to a rock under star spillage. I see
      one who is speechless, a woman,
has just buried her children asleep in a mound of wool.
      Silver currents of breath eddy from
faces small by the fire. She squints into the heart-quaking

ripple of wind. It makes her eyes water for a man absent,
      loved. Once he lifted her bonnet
by a pond and the sun flamingly poured. She felt herself
      charred. Now she wonders what he has
discovered down there in the salt-dark, blinks, shakes it off,

and tries, expressionlessly, to remember a day she pleased
      him. They breasted the snow. He
roared for delight. The white spume was like clouds. She
      feels unlike all others. Her prayer
when it comes, comes wordless. It flickers from fire, star,

and spruce, from the orange head crowns of children
      growing fast. It holds the land, unblooming,
where below she will walk, flinging seed. Hard
      ground waits unhoused like no place.
Why, then, do tears glide? Does she feel she has slipped

under the far black plain of air? On the rock she sits ghostly.
     I, too, have stood and sat
in starless air, dizzied. I could not understand the enormous
     roar like selves disembodied.
And once at my child's window heard it, saw a doe's face

swimming toward me in the yard's snow, ice-legged, and I
     felt at my back some house light
slowly spill into her knowing until she walked it and came
     near and knew me there, all secret.
I put my hand on sealed glass and hand shadow fell into her

living so it lay upon her one great leap. I went with her, in
     dark. Among fliers head-cradled I
see how a moment of joy looks in and out, always untold,
     always known less than fully by anyone
who stands hard on the earth. But how say such a thing

and not turn the worm that night-long lies in the waiting
     hearts? In time we feel ourselves shaken,
bells ring, we strap our bodies down. We look in the dark
     for the place we must descend to.
So much pressure makes us believe we may not be the dreamed ones,

but, more than ever, we are. We remember what we have
     left behind, yet try to think of naming
the little we bring for those we bring ourselves back to. We
     say as we must, everything was just
as dreamed: trees with houses living in their limbs, fish

and fruit to be freely picked, bird song and a horizon
    brilliant as gold snow, a language of song
wonderful as natives whose skins stay honied in the mind,
    and rain pouring like prayer in its wild
surfeit on night sleep. And from bags will come, like selves

promised, dresses of flowered silk, toys, figures slowly
    honed from the visions of a blind
Chinese father, a hand-carved unleaping deer, a chain of
    sweets, coral, snapshots of the black
self-sealed volcano. These ask no explanation and give none.

They unfold the fullness of themselves, they stand in our
    houses, on shelves, face up under stars.
They warn no one of anything, being dreamless, being only
    what shines in the light of the world,
sent down, as we are, into the black ancient lake of air.

BREECH: BIRTH: DREAM

For Dee

---

1. Dog Dreaming

There is always something; and past that something
something else: Jarrell's words lingering
as late in our house the wild skid of a car
overrides the night's news, snow
icing blind the world. I nod
from room to room, remembering
all these somethings come to nothing.

I come to you in your white mound of sleep. My wife, before you
there was no weather, no need to stand mouthing
Jarrell like a bitter nut in the haze
where the TV senselessly snarls
in an elder's malignant voice—

in him I hear the dreamed yawning of the world, I feel
how easily the rafters could fly off, the unlocked
night reach down to touch, as I do, the child
lightless in the unmemory of water.
Someone is ready to go head down
into the sudden scream of self-joy,

                and I feel the shudder like nothing
else in the world slip up my arm. I look above
where nothing is, into flakes, dwarfed
by a blizzard of lice from the world's
savage hump,

and the dog lies
between us, brainlessly clicking her teeth,
her long howl, like a snaking river
in moonlight, its path
taking us into time's dream field

to squat in grass and bite lip
and not cry out, not once,
as the stalks shake
under the enemy's naked feet.

She hunches the floor, the sound of that skull on rock,
the juice of her sex burning at neck stem.
Her flesh pulls taut as a bowstring

as her nails carry her over the floor's field toward us,
you clenched, my hand on your belly, and it comes,
gusting up my arm, the terrible shudder hidden
in you as in a secret of grass.

       At such a moment, almost,
I hear us running, zigzagging low
under leaves already blistered
with blood and dew,
the dream of meat strong in us,
the lure sprung over ground
moon-dazzled like the tip of a spike.

2. Watching an Aircraft Warning Light

Then took back my hand,
went to the window, long crusting,
the road vanished, no tracks,

and watched a warning light pulse on a far tower
that, before snow, was near. It was red.
It blurs pink. Or is gone.

How long have I been here, dreaming—

not far now, I knew, from the first hammering light of dawn.
Love had been red on my face as a bruise.

I thought of that red pulsing light: it would loom up in eyes
flying suddenly out of snow,
blinking, then, over wreckage

like love and mercy. Jarrell
was wrong.

I can feel something pressing on my belly.
Is it you?

3. The Movement of Water at Night

Sometimes you think you can remember the world, even know
why you lie sleepless while through the earth's body
water crawls against rock and is the dream
you want to enter, the black eddy
you jump into

because the blistering vortex of light on the water makes a path
from under your window and climbs onto the bridge
where the water swirls and snaps
like a dreaming dog

and only the heart holds you still. It asks: what is the reason
to be drawn to that drip-drip of nothing?

You have to recite something
or jump. Lost
in a steady fume of snow
I try to say what God is but
say the little I remember, that I have

seen water pound like a dream out of a gorgeous thicket,
and a beaver, insignificant as a shoe, tail-slap
his pond in joy,

and some things I want to name were nothing to me then.
Dawn slicked each leaf silver and, lifting
the Winchester Model 12 pump,
his grandfather's,

a boy believed the gun banged of its own volition, safety broke,
and the echoing blast knocked him ass-backwards.
It looked like he was all that got hit
until he stood at the bottom of the spillway.

The flesh glitters like snow on the green scum of rocks.
Some pieces looked like tits, or parts of.
The water clears itself of streaks

and there ought to be a way to keep a gun, like love, from hurting
even a child trying to enter the world.

I ought to be able to forget that shiny red pulse in the water
and not lie this way listening to the refrigerator
hum over its meat.

If only I could reassemble that joy I might understand
the last hand click of the hall clock,
the red shoe buried in mud and snow,
something the world gives.

All I can do is reach out and touch what's there, licking fingers
to see how hot it is. Getting burnt, anyway.

Is that you, your hand?
Answer me if I'm not dreaming.

I keep my grandfather's gun in the closet. It's worth keeping.
There is much we need to hold onto, *somethings,*
if you want to understand what is trying to pop through
darkness that hums under house roofs and out
of the fine tip ends of grass.

They say you are all right if you can still hear it, the fetal
heart still going pop-pop-pop

like a spillway.

The doc said he wouldn't take chances if he was in that position,
so much is unknown, even televised.
You haven't come far from squatting
and have to be careful
when you bring a child feet first.

And no guarantee because there's always something that shoots
down the program, count on it, and if you push
past that something, something else, but
you shouldn't worry.
Luck's something.

Yes, that's my hand. It's me.
I can feel the movement, the water too.

I can feel the face I'm growing at the back of my eyelids.
It's my grandfather's, the coronary's, grinning
down the sheet at the inexplicable
erection, and the tears

fall down my cheeks
to lodge in your hair grayed by snow spit.
But the light is almost brightening

and I think how, once, I dove too far down in his pond, breathless.
I listened to myself clawing up, bubbling
wordlessly not to let go,
oh, God, don't let go.
The light boiled.

My grandfather said, "Boy, that's where you come from."
He loved my grandmother. He loved me.
At the end he barked like a dog.
He flooded the bed.

He pulled me from his pond feet first.

I know there must be a way to learn to love
even the incontinent waters of old men
and the bloodstain on sheets,
and maybe those people strapped in
for the Christmas descent
count the minutes
until the secret will be exchanged.

4. A Dream of a Jacklighter

Because there are no children in his house, there is nothing
to wake to, crying out.

Because he looks like any father and is not. Imagine him,
long snout of the rifle, a shadow, hunting
at night the image of beauty.

His hand on the cold truck wheel shakes.
His hands in little convulsions
backlit by gauges and numbers
that stare at him like love's
unremembering eyes.

Because for a man like him there is nothing else but the night
that is beyond the last day.

Because the world arranges such meetings: the deer have come,
they stand as if summoned, in grace.
The ice-cobbled road down-spools
under his boots, refusing

to sound like a window opening for the burglar. Light
unalterably leaps from his hand and under it
nothing could change this moment
or blot out the sun god

laying breath on their breath. Because they wait, cornered
in the walls of his will, believers
mostly in darkness, mostly
not choosers or chosen,

accompanying one appointed, for whom grass at hooves slightly stirs.
Her blue eyes cannot explain him, the shot
rocks her
to buckle under his muzzle.

The fawn would nurse his light except for the throat he slits.

Because he must make his dream real in order to remember, some things
cry out in absence and some tearlessly wait.
He wants to know which he is.

Because he must violate the world to know
he is in the world.

We lie in the world, unsleeping in fear, his name on our lips
drawn from the steadily poured haze of the television.
This is how he enters each house

silent as a hill of snow, trying to show what has passed
beautifully through his hands.
He would like to lie down between us.

Because someone here is a carrier of truth he cannot bear,
he would take out his knife like a cold wind
we must hunch at.

This is a definition of joy and beauty.
Not what you think.
He is not what you think.

He is only something in a dream we are the meaning of, something
to be touched like a deep of water,
a fist of snow
where red dawn comes sailing.

5. Final Preparations

I sit in the room swollen with teary light,
cross-legged like an elder,
willing to try anything.
Is this yoga, and why in hell
do I still shiver?

You keep the crib packaged, the toys stacked
in a closet, not even pictures
grace these blind walls.

Anything could happen, something . . .

The red light I kept dreaming all night
ticks over the clean fields
of our country,
over the long veins of rivers

like the road where this morning
we skidded you in safe.
The phone goes on
ringing like our luck

and nothing has happened,
and I can still smell the bacon
where the water broke at your feet.

I think maybe now I can put things together,
if only the phone will stop,
if only I can think
of something

not the flamed face we labored for,
the appalling livid truth that
love is.

1. A Place in the Forest

An opening in thick growth one comes to,
dead end mostly, trail having declined
without your notice, ideas fallen away,
a thick wall of festering luminousness.
For some the deeply scarred bark
whose flesh folds hide moss, life tracks
of the least weasel, a snakeskin.
For others only vines thick-meshed
as family, obligation, that Sunday
when she lifted her hat by the lake.
Even the natural lair of minotaurs.
A darkness hovers beyond, seeping in,
leaves like years are laminated
underfoot, and the sun spirals down
an electric chimney of space. How easy
to feel with the same lost conviction
of faith long folded with Father's hands,
there is no decision now to be made,
no word to be frightened by. Only *here,*
a gently green wind at the dry lips,
recognized by your body that slowly
is pouring itself like oil down.
After this dream of sitting for years,
there is the casual look for hacked
scars of machete, or perhaps that
runneled and rusted lid of a tin can
once slipped painlessly into your heel
now booted and safe. The needle stung,

you limped for a time. Thinking back,
as if each knoll and root were a clue
unapprehended, the trail seems a dream,
but each step so vivid the least blade
must remember and wait to tell someone
you had come. But what name will be given?
Lying in this space you feel you know
what a great-uncle does day-long
in the whining belly of the *Titanic*.
It is not unpleasant but very personal,
like a belief. You are sure no one
waits on the wall's other side. No word
exists beyond but will be yours, fully,
as it was once, when you were a child.
You spoke at last, but they had gone
far off in the absence of the house.
There was only your small pink face
speaking into itself, and the word,
shaped to catch the world, only bodiless,
and Mother's plants hanging like a wall
about to close on the night-black window.
Now there is the lightless beyond again,
one keeps turning to face it, as if
there will always be one more room
in the world, silent just like this,
as if when you arrive there, alone,
it will be exactly as you have wished,
except empty in the towering light,
the kitchen, voices and smell, not right
under the staircase. But you feel easy,
as if standing at the back porch, as if
shutting the gate, latch not forgotten,
to the alley. Already your body gathers

its spilled oil like an old kerchief
pulled from the air's sly pocket,
a memento from an uncle, close-woven,
useful, unstained, coiling at the throat.

2. Tide Pools

At dusk and long-distance they are the mouths
to another world, caves of silence that speak
only in light, and tonight, family packed
for home travel, we take a last, slow route
over sand the sea has been all day cleaning.
At driftwood the children stop, first veering
off wordlessly, and kneel to know some texture
of wood, or stand merely to dream themselves
freely into the gathering shadows of the land.
As we go ahead of them, we imagine their hands
collecting what seems to have waited for each,
shells, starfish, agates like a lover's eyes.
Then we also drift apart, each following deep
runnels the tide has left, and after awhile
I see you hunched on a rock, almost a part of it.

The light is nearly gone and the wind chills me
so I think of my father's whistle, how it called
the sundered shadows of a family into the house.
But do not whistle now, through the lips he made,
for somehow we have come where we may be apart
and whole. Instead, I walk farther to the north,
until you are all taken into shapes of this place.

Then I find it, the deepest pool, rock-vaulted,
light bending and alive in water faintly moving.

I see the lacy deceptions, creatures disguised
as rock whose breath flutes in quick freshets.
A killdeer cries from the dark suck of the surf
and, though sweet, that darkness is not wanted.
This hole is filled with the last golden light
and by it I learn to see what I always suspected—

the small, quiet, incessant outcroppings of life.
For awhile I stare into the spooling depth, for
here are hard black eyes and iron shells, glitter
of hulls laid forever side by side like the dead
unwarily caught at last, perfect and untouchable.

When finally I whistle there is almost no light,
but there's enough. You come, then, invisible,
a sound made by the sand, a mingling of laughter,
and I duck under just in time, holding my breath.
How I love your squeal of delight when I burst up
like a king from underground! Soon we are all in,
all naked, splashing and crying like white birds.
The road home will be long and dark, the stars cold,
but collected, like this, we will be buoyed beyond
the dark snags and splinters of what we once were.

ACKNOWLEDGMENTS

For *Cumberland Station*

The poems "Cumberland Station," "On a Field Trip at Fredericksburg," "The Perspective and Limits of Snapshots," and "Sailing the Back River" were copyrighted in 1975 and "Looking for the Melungeon" (originally "Shack Song"), "Looming: An Address to Matthew Fontaine Maury," and "The Funeral Singer" were copyrighted in 1976, all by The New Yorker Magazine, Inc.

Many of the poems collected here first appeared in the following publications, to whose editors grateful acknowledgment is made for permission to reprint:

Ascent: "The Delivery"; *Carolina Quarterly:* "Si Hugget, Drifting, Ruptured"; *Chariton Review:* "Undertaker, Please Go Slow"; *Chicago Review:* "Pink Slip at Tool and Dye," "Driving Home in the Breaking Season," "With Walt Whitman at Fredericksburg," "In the City of Wind," "The Sex of Poetry"; *Greensboro Review:* "The Cunner in the Calotype"; *Hudson Review:* "One Question, Two Seasons," "The Gift of the Second Snow"; *Jam To-Day:* "Eastern Shore: Smith Island," "The Last Morning"; *Kansas Quarterly:* "The Austringer's Dissertation"; *Kayak:* "The Divorce"; *Midwest Quarterly:* "The Ancestor," "The Testimony of Wine"; *Minnesota Review:* "A Poem While It Is Raining"; *The Nation:* "Lee's Statue: Richmond"; *New Yorker:* "Cumberland Station," "On a Field Trip at Fredericksburg," "Sailing the Back River," "The Perspective and Limits of Snapshots," "The Funeral Singer," "Looming: An Address to Matthew Fontaine Maury," "Looking for the Melungeon" (originally "Shack Song"); *North American Review:* "When the Fiddlers Gather"; *Northwest Review:* "Hole, Where Once in Passion We Swam"; *Ohio Review:* "Small Song for Breadloaf" (originally "The Levitator"); *Perspective:* "The Palmreader"; *Prairie Schooner:* "Something the Wind Says Tonight"; *Poetry:* "Dome Poem"; *Poetry Northwest:* "Blues for Benny Kid Paret"; *Puddingstone:* "Coming Attractions," "How to Get to Green Springs"; *Shenandoah:* "Night Fishing for Blues," "The Luminosity of Life," "Figure from an Elder Lady," "Some Good Luck in Lightfoot"; *Southern Poetry Review:* "Snake Sermon," "Picking Cherries"; *Sou'wester:* "Drunks," "Pietàs: The Petrified Wood," "For the Polioed Girl Killed by Cottonmouths on Her Birthday"; *Windsor Review:* "First Hunt at Smithfield"

For *Goshawk, Antelope*
Many of the poems collected here first appeared in the following publications:

American Poetry Review: "Morning Light: Wanship, Utah," "Hawktree," "Between the Moon and the Sun," "A Moment of Small Pillagers," "Over the Ozarks, Because I Saw Them, Stars Came," "Convulsion," "That Moment, Which You Could Love, What of It"; *Ascent:* "Hospital Memory during Storm," "Antelope Standing, Some Lying," "To Anyone Hunting Agates on a Pacific Beach," "A Fixation with Birds" (part 4 of "The Suicide Eaters"); "Sea Change: The Rented House at Seal Rock, Oregon," "Corner Room, Hog-Scald in the Air," "Loon," "A Gold of Birds," "Night, Our Hands Parting the Blue Air"; *Aura:* "Black Widow"; *Georgia Review:* "Pine Cones"; *Hudson Review:* "Raw Light, Mountain Lake," "The White Holster," "In the Yard, Late Summer"; *Iowa Review:* "The Sound of a Silk Dress," "Under the Scrub Oak, a Red Shoe"; *Ironwood:* "The True Sound of the Goshawk," "A Memory at the Edge of Swollen Rivers"; *The Nation:* "Chinaberry Tree," "Hath the Drowned Nothing to Dream?"; *New Yorker:* "Goshawk, Antelope," "Treehouse," "Waving," "August, on the Rented Farm," "Messenger," "The Roundhouse Voices," "The Collector of the Sun," "Rain Forest"; *North American Review:* "The Dark Eyes of Daughters" (originally "Pickles"); "These Promises, These Lost, in Sleep Remain to Us"; *Poetry:* "Apples in Early October," "Willows, Pond Glitter," "Dreams in Sunlit Rooms"; *Porch:* "Settlement"; *Prairie Schooner:* "The Suicide Eater" (part 1 of "The Suicide Eaters"); "On the Limits of Resurrection" (part 2 of "The Suicide Eaters"); *Quarterly West:* "Playing Ball"; *Three Rivers Poetry Journal:* "Dandelions"; *Western Humanities Review:* "Waking among Horses," "Greenheart Fern," "In Snow, a Possible Life"

For *Dream Flights*
Acknowledgments are due to the editors of the following magazines for first publication of these poems, sometimes under different titles and in different forms:

Atlantic Monthly: "Wildfire"; *New England Review:* "White Beach, Black Beach: Buckroe, Virginia," "Crab"; *New Yorker:* "Mud Holes," "Elegy in an Abandoned Boatyard," "The Colors of Our Age: Pink and Black," "Cleaning a Fish," "Dream Flight"; *Ploughshares:* "Breech: Birth: Dream"; *Poetry:* "Two Poems from Western America"; *Portland Review:* "Artificial Niggers"; *Prairie Schooner:* "The Pornography Box," "The Traveling

Photographer: Circa 1880," "Going Home: Ben's Church, Virginia," "The Water Horse"; *Southern Poetry Review:* "Three Memories from a Southern State" (parts 1 and 2); *Three Rivers Poetry Journal:* "Three Memories from a Southern State" (part 3); *Vanderbilt Poetry Review:* "The Tire Hangs in the Woods"

NATIONAL POETRY SERIES

Eroding Witness
Nathaniel Mackey (1985)
Selected by Michael S. Harper

Palladium
Alice Fulton (1986)
Selected by Mark Strand

Cities in Motion
Sylvia Moss (1987)
Selected by Derek Walcott

The Hand of God and a Few
Bright Flowers
William Olsen (1988)
Selected by David Wagoner

The Great Bird of Love
Paul Zimmer (1989)
Selected by William Stafford

Stubborn
Roland Flint (1990)
Selected by Dave Smith

The Surface
Laura Mullen (1991)
Selected by C. K. Williams

The Dig
Lynn Emanuel (1992)
Selected by Gerald Stern

My Alexandria
Mark Doty (1993)
Selected by Philip Levine

The High Road to Taos
Martin Edmunds (1994)
Selected by Donald Hall

Theater of Animals
Samn Stockwell (1995)
Selected by Louise Glück

The Broken World
Marcus Cafagña (1996)
Selected by Yusef Komunyakaa

OTHER POETRY VOLUMES

Local Men and *Domains*
James Whitehead (1987)

Her Soul beneath the Bone:
Women's Poetry on Breast Cancer
Edited by Leatrice Lifshitz (1988)

Days from a Dream Almanac
Dennis Tedlock (1990)

Working Classics: Poems on
Industrial Life
Edited by Peter Oresick and Nicholas Coles
(1990)

Hummers, Knucklers, and Slow Curves:
Contemporary Baseball Poems
Edited by Don Johnson (1991)

The Double Reckoning of
Christopher Columbus
Barbara Helfgott Hyett (1992)

Selected Poems
Jean Garrigue (1992)

New and Selected Poems, 1962–92
Laurence Lieberman (1993)

The Dig and *Hotel Fiesta*
Lynn Emanuel (1994)

For a Living: The Poetry of Work
Edited by Nicholas Coles and Peter Oresick
(1995)

The Tracks We Leave:
Poems on Endangered Wildlife of North
America (1996)
Barbara Helfgott Hyett